Clay Thompson's

Valley 101

A Slightly Skewed Guide to Living in Arizona

PRIMER
PUBLISHERS

Phoenix, Arizona

Clay Thompson's Valley 101
A Slightly Skewed Guide to Living in Arizona

Primer Publishers
5738 North Central Avenue
Phoenix, Arizona 85012
www.claythompsonbooks.com
info@primerpublishers.com
(800) 521-9221

Cover design by ATG Productions, Inc., Christy Moeller-Masel — www.atgproductions.com
Interior design by The Printed Page, Lisa Liddy — www.theprintedpage.com
Printed by Central Plains Book Manufacturing, Winfield, KS — www.centralplainsbook.com

ISBN 0-935810-71-4

Publisher's Cataloging-in-Publication Data
(Prepared by The Donohue Group, Inc.)

Thompson, Clay.
    Clay Thompson's Valley 101 : a slightly skewed guide to living in Arizona / by Clay Thompson.
    p. cm.
ISBN: 0-935810-71-4
1. American wit and humor—Arizona. 2. Arizona—Humor. 3. Arizona—Social life and customs—Humor. I. Title. II. Title: Valley 101.

PN6162 .T456 2003
818'.5209—dc21

For Madeleine and Elizabeth
My daughters

Contents

Foreword

These are among the things I know:

It's all right to eat crayfish in Arizona but nobody knows for sure why it rains cats and dogs. If you sit in a chair and make clockwise circles with your right foot while drawing the number 6 in the air with your right hand, your foot will change direction.

Armadillos are weird but not just because they are related to sloths; cats can sleep 16 hours a day and are particularly cute during those hours; and there's a store in Sitka, Alaska, that sells wallets made of duct tape.

All these choice pieces of information — and many others like them — have found permanent homes in my mental attic because I am a Clay Thompson fan. Perhaps, even, a groupie. A loyal and faithful groupie. Because every morning of every week, I acquire vast accumulations of knowledge through the words of my kind and gentle master by turning to the back page of the *Arizona Republic*'s B Section. And there, under his patient guidance, I refuel my brain cells by reading "Valley 101," written by the aforementioned Clay Thompson.

While other sections of the paper deal with such inconsequentials as raging wars, sagging economies and sweating athletes, Clay Thompson slogs it out in the trenches of real life, confronting such inconsistencies as nose whistling and scuts. His computer is his sword and with it he slashes away at the myths and lies so commonly associated with excess humidity, magma and monkey dishes.

I am honored, therefore, to be associated with Clay Thompson in this compilation of his work. So honored, in fact, that I propose a Clay Thompson Bobble-Head Doll.

Sam Lowe
August 2003

Acknowledgments

Sam Lowe wrote the introduction to this book! Can you believe it? Wow. Sam Lowe, the long-time B1 columnist for the *Phoenix Gazette*, has written more columns than I've had hot meals. What a guy.

That, however, is neither here nor there. The subject at hand here is this book, which I hope you bought at full price, because I need the money. Maybe you should buy two.

At this point I am, I guess, supposed to do the acknowledgment thing. I could rattle off a long list of colleagues, friends and especially loved ones who have encouraged, inspired, goaded, assisted, advised, yelled at me, whatever, in this endeavor. If I were to do so, I would inevitably omit someone who had been especially helpful to me and that person would then be irked and might not be willing to encourage, inspire, goad, assist, advise or yell in the future. Then where would I be?

So this is a collective thank-you to you all. You know who you are, and you know, I hope, how much I appreciate it. That said, I must especially thank Julia Wallace, who is now the big muckety-muck at the *Atlanta Journal-Constitution*, which I guess is in Georgia, but who was once *The Republic* editor who decided I should be the person to do the column. Thanks a lot.

More than that, I must without fail thank all *The Republic* readers who seem, for whatever reason, to enjoy these columns and who continually send me the questions that are my bread and butter. You people may be odd, but I appreciate you.

What Is This Valley Of The Sun?

June 6, 1999

Q: *Everybody refers to this area as the Valley. What exactly is the Valley the valley of?*

A: This is a deeply troubling question because it actually required some work to nail down the answer.

The easy part first: This is the Valley of the Sun.

Of course it isn't really the Valley of the Sun. The ancient Hohokam Indians did not say to their relatives, "Hey, you should come down to the Valley of the Sun for the winter."

Valley of the Sun was a name cooked up in the 1930s to boost tourism. As these sorts of things go, it's not bad — short, snappy, descriptive.

It's definitely an improvement over "the Denver of the Southwest," which is how the boosters touted Phoenix in the 1890s.

And they could hardly call it "the Valley of Brutal Heat," or the "Valley of the Big Gulp" or the "Valley of Really Expensive Golf Resorts."

So Valley of the Sun works.

But because you cannot live in an advertising slogan, we don't live in the Valley of the Sun. We live in the Salt River Valley.

This is where actual work came in.

What constitutes the Salt River Valley? Where does it begin and where does it end? And if this is the Salt River Valley, why does it look, for the most part, like the Salt River Flats?

The guy in the cubicle across the aisle says the valley of the Salt River begins at the Salt's confluence with the Verde River, a few miles below Saguaro Lake, and ends with the Salt's confluence with the Gila River, which is near Avondale.

However, because we can't base news stories on the opinions of the guy in the cubicle across the aisle, learned advice was sought.

Anthony Brazel, professor of geography at Arizona State University, maintains the valley of the Salt River is the watershed drained by said river — about 6,300 square miles. That's a lot of valley.

You know that old saying: There's never a fluvial geomorphologist around when you need one. Well, it's not true. We found one right away — Will Graf, regents professor of geology at ASU. Fluvial geomorphology, in a nutshell, is the geology of rivers.

Technically, Graf said, Brazel is correct: The valley of the Salt River is that area drained by the Salt.

Then he said a lot of other stuff we didn't understand before offering up this definition: The valley of the Salt could be considered that area in which fluvial materials — rocks or gravel or sand or whatever deposited by the river over the centuries — cover the bedrock.

That area, Graf said, is roughly bounded by South Mountain, the north Scottsdale-Cave Creek area, Granite Reef Dam east of the Salt River Reservation, and the tiny town of Arlington, which is about 50 miles west of downtown Phoenix.

And it's a broad, flat valley because, over the eons, the river wandered all over the place, depositing fluvial material willy-nilly.

Dig down anywhere in that area and you will be digging Salt River fluvial stuff for time immemorial. In some areas, it runs as deep at 15,000 feet, which is a lot of fluvial material.

So, there you have it, we live in the Valley of Salt River Fluvial Deposits, which isn't as catchy as Valley of the Sun but still beats the Denver of the Southwest.

Monsoons
July 4, 1999

Q: *I thought monsoons were something that happened in places like Bangladesh. Why do I keep hearing the TV weather people talk about the monsoon here?*

A: Because you have the sound on. If you turned the sound off, you wouldn't hear them at all and you could still see the temperature and stuff on the screen. It wouldn't be so confusing. Or annoying.

Monsoon comes from an Arabic word, mawsim, which means "season." It is usually taken to mean weather brought on by a seasonal change in the winds, and that's just what happens in Arizona.

Every year, generally in late June or early July, atmospheric conditions combine to push the jet stream to the north. This allows winds to flow into the state from the south or southeast. These winds carry a lot of moisture from the Gulf of California and the Gulf of Mexico.

This humid air means:

(A) Your evaporative cooler isn't going to be as effective as it was when the air was dry.

(B) There probably will be a lot of storms, some of them quite loud and nasty.

(C) You should go to San Diego and stay there until sometime in mid-September.

There probably will be a lot of storms because when that moist, cool air from the south hits hot air radiating up off the desert floor, it creates a witch's cauldron of towering clouds that usually reaches the boiling point in the late afternoon or early evening.

These storms can be powerful, and they can be dangerous. The winds can be fearsome and the lightning spectacular. (Be careful: A couple of years ago, up in the mountains, a man was relieving himself on a pine tree when the tree was struck by lightning. He survived, but can you imagine?)

These storms also have a tendency to hit the East Valley first, and often hardest, for the simple reason that they generally come from the east and because the East Valley is closest to the mountains where the storms often breed.*

After months of featureless weather, these storms also can be quite entertaining.

It's not unusual to drive through a neighborhood and see everyone sitting out front on lawn chairs watching the lightning dance across the sky over another part of town. Or maybe they're sitting outside because the power is out. Whatever, monsoon storms are a good chance to meet the neighbors.

And we need the rain. The Valley usually gets about one-third of its annual rainfall during the monsoon season. This year, with rainfall already off an inch and a quarter, we really need it.

The monsoon doesn't last forever — it just seems that way. It usually breaks sometime in middle or late September, and then things go back to being plain old hot for a few more weeks.

Pray we don't get a repeat of 1984, when the monsoon lasted a record 99 days.

If this is your first monsoon, buck up and make the most of it. Like a lot of Arizona, it really can be quite beautiful in a way — the clouds and the lightning and the winds.

Just be careful. Stay away from pine trees.

*This is not, umm, exactly 100% true. See the question on page 12 and just forget you read this sentence, OK?

Canals
July 11, 1999

Q: *What are the canals for, and how do they work?*
A: Bibbity, bobbity boo. Next question, please.
Oh, all right, we'll tell you: Farms and gravity.
Really.

The miles and miles of canals maintained by the Salt River Project were put there to bring water to thirsty acres of alfalfa, cotton, citrus and dates. Although there are a few pumping stations along the way, nearly all the system operates on the principle that water flows downhill.

That's what worked for the Hohokam, who dug the first canals about 1,300 years ago to water their corn, beans and squash.

The ancient ones had quite a little civilization going — check out the Pueblo Grande Museum in east Phoenix — before they vanished about 500 years ago, probably chased off by a long drought. By the time the Europeans arrived, the desert had reclaimed the Hohokams' 135 miles of canals.

In 1867, Jack Swilling, a former Confederate soldier living in Wickenburg, realized what those lines in the sand meant. He formed the Swilling Irrigation Canal Co. and dredged out one of the canals. A meager harvest resulted and — voila! — agriculture was reborn in the Valley, and Phoenix had a reason for being.

The subsequent flood of farmers expanded and improved the canal system, but they lacked what the Hohokam had lacked: a way to tame the Salt, which actually had water in it in those days. The problem was, it either had too much water or not enough.

Enter the Salt River Project, an interesting animal. It is really two entities: the Salt River Valley Water Users Association and the Salt River Project Agricultural Improvement and Power District.

This gets a little confusing, so pay attention. The water side of SRP is a private corporation. The electric side of SRP is a political subdivision of the state of Arizona. That's why, depending on what part of town you live in, you find candidates for the board of directors on the ballot when you go to vote for governor or county supervisor.

The Water Users Association was founded in 1903 by landowners who wanted the feds to build a dam on the Salt. They basically pledged their land against the cost of building Roosevelt Dam, which was completed in 1911 and named for President Teddy Roosevelt, who had signed the enabling legislation and turned up for the dedication.

(Amazing true fact: The first water over the spillway of the new dam was bottled and used to christen the USS *Arizona*, which met an untimely end at Pearl Harbor.)

Anyway, in 1937, when the Depression was making it tough for farmers to meet the debt payments for the dam (which wasn't paid off until 1955), the Legislature established the power side of SRP as a political subdivision of the state. That enabled the district to sell tax-free municipal bonds to help pay off the dam debt.

If you live within the boundaries of the SRP's water district, which are not necessarily the same as the power district's boundaries, you get SRP irrigation water from the canals. That's why in some older parts of the Valley you see berms built up around the lawns — to hold in the irrigation water.

Of course, growing Bermuda grass wasn't what the canals were built for, but most of the cropland that once covered the Valley has given way to houses and Home Depots.

The major canals actually are owned by the federal government, but maintained by SRP. They are mostly controlled today by computers and remote sensors, but in the old days, keeping the canals flowing was the job of zanjeros — ditch riders — who patrolled the canal system. Some irrigation services still call their workers zanjeros.

Now the real newcomer question — the one you're too embarrassed to ask: Where does the water come from?

In the years after construction of Roosevelt Dam, a series of five dams — three on the Salt and two on the Verde — were built to help store water from the rivers' 13,000-square-mile watersheds.

Those dams created the various lakes — Canyon, Saguaro, etc. — where you go to fish or water-ski.

That's why there's no water in the Salt — not counting Tempe's new Town Lake: It's all damned up upstream. The water enters the SRP canal system at the Granite Reef Diversion Dam below the confluence of the Salt and Verde in the far East Valley.

And that is why, even though you came here to get away from the snow, you should care how much snow falls in Arizona's central and eastern mountains. That snowmelt keeps the lakes filled.

The watershed is not the Valley's sole source of water. SRP and various cities pump groundwater and the Central Arizona Canal, a huge undertaking, delivers Arizona's share of Colorado River water to the Valley and Tucson.

Scorpions

July 18, 1999

Q: *Help! My house is overrun with scorpions, and I hate them.*

A: How ungracious of you. First of all, the scorpions were here first, and secondly, they absolutely adore you. And what do they get from you? The back of your Reebok.

And, in a way, it's your fault there are so many of them in the first place. Well, not your fault personally, but our fault collectively.

There are about 35 species of scorpions in Arizona, but only five or six in the Phoenix area, including our personal favorite, the giant hairy scorpion.

All are venomous. That's their stock-in-trade. But according to Marilyn Bloom, a microbiology research specialist at Arizona State University, there is only one species that really needs concern us: the bark scorpion.

This is a nasty little critter, skinny and yellowish in color, and it's sting can cause intense pain, numbness and, at least in theory, death. Bloom said there are no accounts of anyone dying of a scorpion sting in the 40 years that records have been kept.

Bloom has an interesting job. With the help of three goats, she produces scorpion antivenin for distribution to area hospitals, doctors and veterinarians. During the summer, she gets a dozen or so requests for antivenin a week.

Here's how to tell if your scorpions are bark scorpions: Only bark scorpions climb vertical surfaces. If your scorpions confine themselves to scurrying along the floor, you're probably OK. If you're finding them on the walls or in your drapes or climbing up the side of your house (or your leg), you've got a problem.

There are scorpions all over the Valley, but many of us have gone for years without ever seeing one, much less getting stung.

Some people believe they are more common in areas where new housing is encroaching on the scorpions' natural desert habitat. That's only partly true, according to Bert Putterman, general manager of Arizona Exterminating Co.

On a hunk of untouched desert, the scorpion count may be relatively low, Putterman said, "but when a development comes in, suddenly there might be thousands to an acre."

That's because when houses and humans show up, "it's just like a Furr's Cafeteria moved in" to scorpions, he said.

"Scorpions are extremely environmentally compatible with us," Putterman said.

That's because humans come bearing gifts, mostly scorpion food and shelter.

Our security lights and streetlights attract bugs, which, in turn, attract scorpions. Our rock gardens and woodpiles and laundry rooms and well-watered lawns provide shelter and water. We're the best thing that ever happened to scorpions.

So, as the urban area grows, so does the scorpion population.

"Twenty years ago, when I first moved here, we'd get three or four calls a summer for scorpions, and we'd go out on them just as a novelty," Putterman said.

"Ten years ago, we could identify specific areas of infestation (around the Valley.) Today, 75 percent of the calls we get are for scorpions."

If you do have scorpions in your house, it's probably not by their choice. Scorpions are most comfortable in conditions 75 to 95 degrees, Putterman said, and chances are the coolness of your house makes them sluggish. They'd just as soon be outside, perhaps under that nice cool damp towel your kids left on the lawn after they played in the sprinkler.

Because scorpions are nocturnal and most exterminators are not, spraying them probably isn't going to have much effect. Short of a direct hit, most pesticides don't really bother scorpions much. On the other hand, spraying will kill their food source, bugs.

But killing the bugs might not make that much difference. Bloom says a healthy scorpion can go nine to 12 months without eating. That means a bark scorpion would be perfectly content to curl up in the toe of a seldom-worn shoe for months on end.

Putterman and Bloom offered a number of tips for keeping scorpions away:

- Switch your outdoor lights from white bulbs to yellow. Yellow light doesn't attract bugs the way white light does.

- Check your weather-stripping. If you can slide a business card under your weather-stripping, there's enough room for a scorpion to wiggle through.

- Caulk or otherwise plug the spaces where electrical, phone or waterlines enter your house. Ditto in the kitchen and bathrooms where pipes come out of the wall.

- Clear away, or at least frequently move, woodpiles or any other stuff you might have stacked up near your house.

- Don't leave wet towels on the ground around a pool or spa. Conversely, if you want to catch scorpions, leave a damp towel on your kitchen floor overnight. In the morning, pick it up, with tongs or with gloves on, and see what came calling.

- The redwood bark some folks use as mulch looks nice on flowerbeds, but it's a scorpion magnet. If you're digging around it, wear gloves and keep your eyes open.

Airport

September 26, 1999

Q: *Why, when you drive into Phoenix Sky Harbor International Airport, is there a sign that says there are three terminals: 2, 3 and 4? Where I come from, we started counting at "one."*

A: That sign just nags at you every time you see it, doesn't it? It's like a picture that isn't quite straight or like sitting across from someone with a loose thread on their cuff: You just have to fix it.

There is a perfectly good reason for the terminal-numbering system. Actually, it isn't perfectly good, but it will have to do.

And if you think it's silly now, there is a possibility that in the far distant future, we will only have two terminals — 4 and 5.

First, some history. Time was, children, when we actually had a Terminal 1. It stood a bit west of Terminal 2. It opened in 1952 and was a big deal at the time. Its restaurant, which for a time barred Blacks, was described as "a symphony in chrome, leather and soft-toned wood." People actually went to the airport to eat. Can you imagine?

Terminal 1 was Terminal Only until 1962, when Terminal 2 opened. There was almost immediately talk of tearing down Terminal 1, but it hung on until 1991, when it was razed shortly after Terminal 4 opened. At which point we were left with terminals 2, 3 and 4.

The city last year spent about $2.5 million redoing all the signage at the airport, and that would have seemed like a pretty good time to renumber the terminals as 1, 2 and 3. But Bob Petrillo, an Aviation Department engineer who worked on the new signs, said that after all those years, new numbers wouldn't have worked.

"I think that would have caused even more confusion. So many people know, for instance, that America West is in Terminal 4, and that building is Terminal 4," Petrillo said.

The long-range plan, according to Petrillo, calls for a big new terminal and destruction of Terminal 3.

Under the current logic, we would then have a sign that read "There are two terminals: 4 and 5," but Petrillo said it is more likely that they would be known as the East and West terminals.

Q: *Why do the monsoon storms seem to hit the East Valley harder than other parts of the area? Does God have something against Mesa?*

A: God was not available for comment, and Scriptures are silent on the question of his feelings about Mesa or the East Valley in general.

However, it seems unlikely, what with everything else he or she must have to do, that the Supreme Being would take time to steer a few thunderstorms at the East Valley.

And besides, it's not true that the East Valley is any more affected by bad — or good — weather than any other parts of town.

Since the monsoon storms come from the east or southeast, the East Valley might be first hit, but not necessarily hardest hit. And even first-hit is an iffy contention.

"It's the same reason that if you flip a coin it comes up heads half the time and tails half the time," said Bill Estle, a meteorologist with the National Weather Service in Phoenix. "It's just a chance thing."

The big storm that dropped a microburst on east Mesa on Sept. 19 wasn't even a monsoon storm, in that it came from the north and west, rather than the east. Mesa just happened to be in the wrong place at the wrong time.

Painted Citrus

October 5, 1999

Q: *Why do people paint the trunks of their citrus trees white?*

A: HA! At last, a question we actually knew the answer to without having to look it up or ask somebody. It's to protect them from the sun. We are sooooo smart.

To celebrate, we asked an actual newcomer in the office if she knew why citrus trunks are painted white, and she said it was to repel insects. These comical newcomers. We were going to laugh at her until we remembered she is much higher up the food chain than us and holds what passes for our career in her elegant and well-manicured hands. So we didn't laugh.

Just to double-check, and to look busy, we called Ralph Backhaus, a professor of plant biology at Arizona State University.

"It's to prevent sunburn," Backhaus said. "It's really important when the trees are young."

Citrus trees have relatively thin bark. Left to their own, they grow more like a shrub than a tree, with shoots growing up at the base and covering the trunk. Without that shading, they need the protection of paint.

Once the canopy of the tree is thick and broad enough to shade the trunk the paint isn't necessary, Backhaus said, but most people keep doing it anyway because they like the way it looks.

You can buy white trunk paint, but just plain old latex house paint will do. Don't use oil-based paint — it will seep into the wood and poison the tree.

You can also, if you choose, buy trunk wraps — burlap or woven polyethylene that will protect a young tree.

Speaking of trees, you know what really frosts Backhaus' keister? Well, he didn't actually say this frosts his keister, but he did say it's one of the biggest landscaping mistakes people make around here — big, cheap trees.

Bargain hunters often buy large trees that have been growing so long in containers that the roots are all jammed up and form "corkscrews,"

Backhaus said. The reason they're big and cheap is that nobody bought them when they were small and more expensive and they just kept growing in the container.

After they're transplanted, the roots begin to grow, but because of their corkscrew shape they eventually just strangle themselves and the tree slowly dies. (This doesn't apply to palm trees, which have different kinds of roots.)

"They'll look good for two or three years and then they'll just die," Backhaus said. "People think it's air pollution or some kind of mystery disease, but it isn't, and these are the ones that tend to blow over in the storms."

Daylight Savings

October 24, 1999

Q: *Why don't we have daylight-saving time in Arizona?*

A: Ah, this is an excellent question. Daylight-saving time is an issue that sums up everything you really need to know about Arizona, namely that we are a contrary people and that it's really, really hot here.

Daylight-saving time is one of those old standby issues that pops up every now and again, usually when the Legislature runs out of dumb ideas. They will argue about it for a while and then, refreshed and re-energized, think of a new dumb idea. It's sort of like cleansing your palate between courses.

Daylight-saving time "adds" an extra hour of sunlight from April through October. It is meant to give you an extra hour for recreation and fun, wholesome or otherwise. We were once told that the driving force behind the federal Uniform Time Act of 1967 was the charcoal briquette industry. We don't know if this is true.

Anyway, as you may have noticed, we already have quite a bit of daylight in Arizona as it is, and it is daylight that tends to be on the warmish side. The idea of adding an extra hour of summer heat doesn't make much sense.

This is not to say we haven't tried it. In 1967, when the Uniform Time Act took effect, Arizona had a six-month fling with DST. Electric meters whirled like tops as people cranked up their air-conditioners during the extra hour of sunshine. Parents complained about tucking their tykes in while the sun was still shining. Owners of restaurants and drive-in movie theaters hated it. In general, it just made everybody grumpy, with the exception of bankers and stockbrokers, who liked being an hour closer to East Coast institutions.

Also, if you ever went back and read all the clippings and letters to the editor from past DST debates, you would find a certain spirit of "By gum, we don't need a bunch of highfalutin Eastern sissy-boy bureaucrats telling us what time it is" running through them. We're just ornery that way.

Bear in mind that a fair-size portion of Arizona does observe daylight-saving time. On the Navajo Reservation, clocks spring forward in April and fall back in October to keep the Arizona piece of the reservation in line with Navajo territory in Utah and New Mexico. But, with typical Arizona contrariness, state offices on the reservation abide by Phoenix time, while federal offices keep daylight-saving time. It makes for some confusion.

Actually, 1967 was not our first experiment in fiddling with the clocks. Along with the rest of the nation, Arizona observed DST during World War II.

And for about 20 years around the turn of the century, Phoenix had its own time zone, a half-hour between Mountain Standard Time and Pacific Standard Time. The Southern Pacific railway operated its trains on Pacific time, and the Santa Fe railroad used Mountain time, so Phoenix and Maricopa County officials decided in the late 1800s to split the difference.

A newspaper story at the time opined, "The majority of the people don't care what kind of time they have, just so they have as much of it as anyone else."

Concrete Walls
November 2, 1999

Q: *What is it with the "wall phenomenon" around here? Who invented the idea of backyard concrete-block fences and why?*

A: Funny you should ask.

We are just back from a trip to the ancestral estate in the Midwest, and one of the first things our charming traveling companion asked — after she asked why Grandma didn't get MTV — was why nobody had fences around their yards.

We were taken aback by her question, because we hadn't really noticed until she asked. (We were also taken aback by a rather alarming shortage of pie in Grandma's refrigerator, cupboards, car, closet, under the beds and everywhere else we looked, and we are wondering if, in addition to not rocking out on MTV, the sainted woman has abandoned rhubarb. We had to make do with cookies.)

Anyway, your query was on our desk when we got back, and we immediately called Max Underwood, a professor of architecture at Arizona State University, who is really, really smart and whose specialty is Valley architecture, and we riddled him your riddle.

Thus spake Underwood:

"If you traveled in the Southwest, if you went to Santa Fe or Tucson or the older areas where there was Spanish influence, there were walls. The walls were there for protection of livestock or for safety, but they were low walls so you could see over them.

"What transpired here in the Phoenix area is that many of the building codes and zoning regulations require these walls" for privacy, safety and to hamper the spread of fire.

Plus, a lot of homeowners' associations require concrete-block fences, presumably for privacy — to keep you from seeing what's going on in your neighbor's back yard or to spare your neighbor from seeing what's going on in your back yard.

Walls are a Valley — or at least Southwest — kind of thing.

"If you went to Southern California," Underwood said, "you would find more chain-link fences or wood fences with vegetation or things that blended more with the landscape. Out here, you get The Wall."

Valley Fever
November 21, 1999

Q: *I have lived in the Valley for two years now and love it. A couple of weeks ago I heard about Valley fever for the first time. What exactly is it?*

A: It would be nice to report that Valley fever is a disease named for our very own Valley, something we could all be proud of, but unfortunately this is not the case. It is named for the San Joaquin Valley in California.

We know this because when your question came in we went to the Internet, and with just a few keystrokes, through the miracle of cybertechnology, we were immediately connected to a Web site offering to show us pictures of teenaged nymphomaniac nurses.

Blushing deeply, we eventually found our way to www.arl.arizona.edu/vfce, which is the Web site of the University of Arizona's Valley Fever Center for Excellence, which, as you would expect, is just chock-full of excellent information about Valley fever, plus some fairly disgusting full-color pictures of what it can do to various body parts, including your spleen.

Valley fever officially is known as coccidioidomycosis. It is a lung disease caused by a fungus found in the soil of areas with low rainfall, high summer temperatures and mild winters. In other words, it is present in most of Arizona.

The experts guess that at least one-third of us have had Valley fever, which you can have without ever realizing it. About 60 percent of the people who get it either have no symptoms or just feel like they have the flu. Symptoms include fatigue, cough, chest pain, fever, rash, headaches and joint aches.

This is not to say it is to be taken lightly. Valley fever can bring on pneumonia, can cause painful bumps on the shins or elsewhere. It can also cause lung damage that looks like cancer on X-rays and can require surgical repair. About 1 percent of cases prove fatal.

People whose jobs involve dirt — farmers, construction workers, archaeologists — have a higher risk of infection than others, but a good dust storm can bring the fungal spores directly to you in the comfort of your own home.

Men are more likely to catch it than women, and many animals can get it, too. Dogs are especially susceptible.

One of the disease's only redeeming values is that second infections are rare. If you do get it, you probably won't get it again.

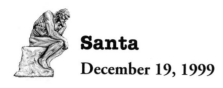

Santa
December 19, 1999

Today, students, to mark the holidays, we are suspending our usual class in favor of Story Hour.

So gather in the glow of the red chile pepper Christmas lights, kiddies, to hear one of our all-time favorite Arizona Christmas stories. No need to take notes, this will not be on the final.

This comes from *A Mile in His Moccasins*, a charming book of Arizona remembrances by Don Dedera, Arizona historian and former editor of *Arizona Highways*.

It concerns one John C. McPhee, who in 1930 was editor of the *Mesa Journal-Tribune*, and who, as the Christmas season neared that year, was concerned about the lagging interest in the city's annual pre-Christmas parade.

"McPhee's plan," Dedera wrote, "deserved some of the superlatives that Hollywood later would tag to fiction. He arranged to have a barnstormer parachute from an airplane at the edge of town. Dressed in a Santa suit, the chutist would then ride in a car at the front of the parade."

But when the time came, the barnstormer was too drunk to jump. McPhee hurried to a clothing store, grabbed a window dummy dressed as Santa and sped to the airport with a new plan. He strapped a parachute on the mannequin and instructed the pilot to pull the ripcord and push the dummy out over a Mesa field. McPhee would hurry to the site, put on the Santa suit and lead the parade himself.

"Mesa's response to the Santa stunt surpassed even McPhee's wildest hopes," Dedera wrote. "The streets were filled with excited celebrants and shoppers. Children climbed atop buildings, scurried up telephone poles, begged to be held aloft by parents. A fever of anticipation gripped the crowd as the airplane circled Mesa once, twice, three times."

Santa appeared in the door of the plane. He fell into the air. The chute did not open. Santa dropped through the sky like an anvil.

Dedera: "When McPhee returned to Mesa the streets were empty, except for a few stunned merchants, transfixed in the doorways of their deserted stores. From homes came the wails of many children. The brave parade wound through downtown Mesa, and there were more marchers than watchers. So great was the shock, a pregnant woman began her labor, and to McPhee's eternal relief, mother and babe were saved.

"McPhee left town for three days."

For as long as 30 years afterward, he was remembered as "the man who killed Santa Claus."

Merry Christmas. Class dismissed.

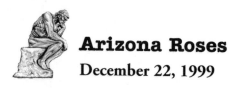

Arizona Roses
December 22, 1999

Q: *Around Cotton Lane and Northern Avenue there are acres and acres of rosebushes. What's the story?*

A: When your question came in we had a good laugh because we assumed you were a comical newcomer who couldn't tell a rosebush from a cotton plant, and we prepared to write a lesson full of smug, condescending remarks covered with a thin veneer of facts about the Arizona cotton industry.

It turned out the joke was on us, which is not an unusual state of affairs, because in calling around we discovered that Arizona is a major producer of rose plants, most of them grown in the northwest Valley near Luke Air Force Base.

Who knew?

And this is not a new thing. It's been going on for 40 years or so.

These are not cut roses, like you would send to your sweetie, but rose plants, like you would buy at a nursery to replant in your yard.

"There are five major growers (in the northwest Valley) and they grow approximately 45 percent of the roses consumed in the United States," said Frank Waterhouse, manager of one of those five producers, Bickman Farms in Litchfield Park.

Most of the other 55 percent are grown around Bakersfield, California.

Waterhouse declined to talk about Bickman Farms' production figures, but said the farm turns out 270 varieties of roses.

"The soil and the climate are the basic factors," said John Hutton, rose production manager for Santa Lucia Farms in El Mirage. "We have a long growing season, which allows field production of roses to be economically feasible."

Hutton said Santa Lucia has 400 varieties and every year plants about 3.5 million (who knew?) rose plants on about 180 acres.

It takes about two years to grow a decent rose plant. They are trimmed, either by machine or by hand, several times during the growing period, and when the harvest comes — right now is the harvest season — a machine with two U-shaped blades goes through the fields, uprooting the plants. Workers follow the machine, pulling out the plants, grading and bundling them.

Refrigerated trucks carry millions of roses from Maricopa County to wholesale and retail nurseries all over the country.

Who knew?

Original Bethany Home Was Early 1900s Tuberculosis Sanitarium

January 2, 2000

Q: *I admit that I'm not new to the Valley, but I have a burning question which in all my 36 years, I cannot answer. How did Bethany Home Road get its name? Is there such a place as "Bethany Home"? I can understand how Camelback, Washington, Central, Indian School and just about all the other major thoroughfares got named, but not Bethany Home. Do you know?*

A: Do we know? Do we know? Do you think the state's largest newspaper, a powerful media colossus such as Phoenix Newspapers Inc., a newspaper for the new millennium, would blithely hand over the awesome responsibility of teaching the Valley 101 course to someone who didn't know something as simple as that?

It is to laugh. Ha, ha.

Actually, no, we don't know. Or at least we didn't know until we asked around a bit.

We did know this much: It had something to do with tuberculosis.

Tuberculosis used to be a big business in Arizona. Around the turn of the century — you know, it just occurred to us that we can't say that anymore without saying which century — tuberculosis patients routinely were sent to Arizona to be cured by the clean, dry air. Sometimes this worked and sometimes it didn't.

The Sunnyslope area — which then was well north of the Phoenix city limits — was the site of many tuberculosis sanitariums, and Scottsdale was once known as "White City" because of all the white tents where the tuberculosis patients lived.

The historian Marshall Trimble told us this when we called up to ask him the Bethany Home question. He knows everything. He knows Dick Lynch, who is a Valley historian who actually knew the answer to the Bethany Home question.

According to Lynch, the Bethany Home was a tuberculosis sanitarium operated in the early 1900s by a religious organization "way out in the boondocks" near what is now 15th Avenue and Bethany Home Road. Hence, the name.

Bethany, as you know, is an ancient town near Jerusalem at the foot of the Mount of Olives. In Hebrew, it means roughly "house of late-season green figs," according to our dictionary.

And while we're on the subject, for any really, really new newcomers, Indian School Road takes its name from a boarding school for Native Americans that the federal government operated at Central Avenue and Indian School Road until 1990. Much of the site is slowly being converted into a city park.

Possible Sunshine
January 13, 2000

Oooooo, weather wonks, have I got one for you today. It's a factoid. A weather factoid. I know you people: This is going to make your toes curl involuntarily, and it may induce a slight flush in some of you.

You're going to love this. It's obscure, it's a uniquely Valley weather factoid, and it's almost but not quite a record.

Go get your scissors and make sure you have change for the copying machine over at the drugstore, because you're going to copy this and send it to friends in other cities. You really can't help yourselves, can you?

OK, here it is: According to the National Weather Service, the average percentage of possible sunshine for 1999 in Phoenix was 93 percent.

You're loving it, aren't you?

Phoenix's 30-year average for possible sunshine is 86 percent, so 1999, boosted by the long dry spell at the end of the year, was an unusually sunny year.

By comparison, the annual average percentage of possible sunshine for Miami is 73 percent. It's 46 percent in Seattle, 54 percent in Chicago and 57 percent in Philadelphia.

Percentage of possible sunshine is measured by a gizmo called a solarimeter. The figure represents the daily amount of sunshine divided by the total available. For instance, if on a winter day there were eight hours of sunshine possible and the sun shone for six hours, the number would be 75 percent.

A percentage for 1998 wasn't available. In 1997, the average was 88 percent.

The Phoenix record for percentage of available sunshine is 94 percent, set in 1960 and tied in 1989. The lowest on record was 75 percent in 1935.

This I learned when I finally stumbled onto the home page of Randy Cerveny, an associate professor of geography at Arizona State University.

Check this out: http://geography.asu.edu/rcerveny. Wander around in there for a while and sooner or later you're going to find every Valley weather factoid you could dream of, as well as links to even more sites.

He has, for instance, weather satellite photos, hourly Arizona readings, a Palmer drought index map, average temperatures and precipitation chances for major holidays and the times, dates and descriptions of every tornado or funnel cloud spotted in the Phoenix area from 1955 to 1990.

Did you know the Phoenix record for most consecutive days with 0.0 percent sunshine is three — Nov. 22-24, 1965? Cerveny did.

Weather wonks: Cerveny is your god; fall to your knees and worship him.

In Heyday Of Oaters, Studio Gave Name To Neighborhood

January 30, 2000

Q: *I recently moved to the area of 40th Street and Camelback Road and my new neighbors tell me it's the Cudia neighborhood, but I can't seem to find out the origin of the name. Can you help?*

A: Here at the gleaming research laboratories of Valley 101, teams of white-coated technicians pored over your question night and day for weeks before reaching the conclusion that maybe we should just ask somebody else.

So we asked the estimable Gus Walker, a *Republic* artist and student of Valley history, who soon produced a tattered copy of *The Golden Days of Theaters in Phoenix* by one Jerry Reynolds in which we found the answer to your question.

The book is a little fuzzy on the dates, but at some time in the late 1930s or early '40s, Salvatore Cudia, "a longtime showman in Europe and Los Angeles," built Cudia City, the Valley's first motion picture studio, near Camelback and 40th Street.

Cudia City turned out such film classics as *Phantom Pinto, Buzzie Rides the Range, Let Freedom Ring* and *Trail City.* After World War II, the Red Ryder movies, starring Wild Bill Elliot, were filmed there.

According to Reynolds, "filming at Cudia City reached its zenith with *26 Men*, a Western series for television. But when cars, planes and utility poles of the city's growth reached the studios, they prohibited outdoor shooting."

Cudia City became a tourist attraction, restaurant and theater before it was torn down to make way for residential development.

Hot Topic Needs Legislative Action

February 15, 2000

As long as our state lawmakers are taking time to thoughtfully draft legislation to protect us from coed dorms and federal martial law and other terrors that keep so many of us awake at night, perhaps they could come up with some laws on a few other bothersome matters.

For instance, the weather. Sure, it's nice right now, albeit a bit dry, but face it: It's just way too hot here in the summer. Some people like hot weather, but I think most of us would agree that by September or so, it ought to start cooling off a bit.

What do you hear people talking about all summer? The need to teach firearms safety in public schools or how hot it is?

A Legislature that really listens to the voice of the people would pass a law mandating no temperatures over 90 after Sept. 15, and while they're at it, they could do something about the monsoon humidity. And dust storms.

As long as they're on weather, our lawmakers could pass a bill requiring that, henceforth, the temperatures at Phantom Ranch at the bottom of the Grand Canyon will be the same as the temperature readings on the South Rim, despite an elevation difference of 5,000 feet or so.

This admittedly is a special-interest bill on behalf of *The Republic*, which can't seem to get the Phantom Ranch readings right to save its flinty soul.

On Sunday, for instance, the very day I ran a column bewailing this problem, we reported the high Saturday at Phantom Ranch had been a scorching 423 degrees. Fahrenheit, I guess.

This alarmed a number of our readers, who either are concerned about a sudden spike in global warming or who had friends or loved ones in the Phantom Ranch area over the weekend.

And another thing: Trout should be required by law to be more cooperative. After all, many Arizona trout are raised in state hatcheries, fed at state expense and then transported in state trucks to streams and lakes that are fished by tax-paying anglers with traditional Judeo-Christian values.

Here's some more proposed legislation certain to win wide support among all outdoor-loving and right-thinking Arizonans:

It's time something is done about the Echo Canyon Trail on Camelback Mountain. It's too steep. According to my guide book, there is a rise in elevation of about 1,400 feet from the trail head to the summit, a direct infringement on my right to have knees that don't crack and pop.

Now, I would never propose that the Legislature physically change the slope of Camelback Mountain, although I wouldn't put it past them. I do suggest we get a new law declaring that, henceforth, the rise in elevation is only 500 feet. This would make some of us at least feel better about the 1.2-mile climb.

One more thing: I have in my hand, my fellow Arizonans, an e-mail from a reader who says he has determined that local noon — the time at which the sun is at its daily zenith — is really 12:40 p.m.

Or something like that. I don't know. I haven't really checked it out yet, but petty details like that shouldn't stand in the way of a law declaring that noon is at noon, just the way God intended it to be when he created every single thing in the universe in just six days, including trout, the Grand Canyon and Arizona legislators.

Stars Reflect Past Glory Of The San Carlos

February 27, 2000

Q: *What is the meaning of the stars with the names of old celebrities in them on the sidewalk at the northwest corner of Central Avenue and Monroe Street?*

A: This was a deeply disturbing question, not because of the stars themselves, but because we had to get up off our pert little butt and actually walk over there and check it out.

And it occurred to us that we had trod that very stretch of sidewalk hundreds of times and never noticed the stars before.

The stars — eight of them — are a reflection of the past glory of the Hotel San Carlos, 202 N. Central Ave., which is still a very nice hotel, but at one time was Phoenix's premier hostelry.

And when Hollywood stars were in town, that's where they stayed. After all, it offered elevators and "automatic cooled air," a kind of forerunner of air-conditioning, and ice-water spigots in the rooms.

The stars in the sidewalk were put in in 1993 to commemorate the visits of luminaries of their day such as Kay Starr, Gene Autry, Tex Beneke, Les Brown, Jean Harlow, Harry James, Mae West and Clark Gable.

The San Carlos was completed in 1927 and was built on the site of Phoenix's first school, an adobe building built in 1874. Dwight B. Heard — as in Heard Museum — financed the project.

For many years, it was where the Valley's in crowd crowded in for lodging, dinner or dancing. It was famous for its onion soup.

The hotel was renovated in 1955 and today still retains many of its original architectural and design touches. Even one of the two original elevators still works and in the basement — and still working — is the well from the old school building.

One last thing — the San Carlos is said to be haunted. In 1928, a young woman, unlucky in love, jumped off the roof of the seven-story hotel to her death. She was wearing an evening gown, and every now and then someone will say they have seen the gauzy form of a woman in the hotel's hallways and felt unexplained breezes.

And the ghosts of three young boys — perhaps spectral truants from the old schoolhouse — have been heard running through the halls, laughing.

Vision Of Downtown Phoenix Is Subject To Change

March 12, 2000

Q: *Why does Phoenix seem to have two downtowns — one "downtown" and then another grouping of high-rises farther north along Central Avenue?*

A: Because many years ago, the city fathers and mothers thought big.

Unfortunately, they also thought wrong, or at least incorrectly. The result is today we have a downtown downtown and downtown uptown, although we know of people who think of anything south of Northern Avenue as being practically the inner city.

According to Dave Reichert, head of the Phoenix Planning Department, back in the 1960s, when we only had one downtown and it was downtown, the city's leaders had dreams of grandeur.

"They wanted to create a new downtown, almost like a Manhattan, and they expanded the (core area) all the way to Camelback Road between Seventh Avenue and Seventh Street," Reichert said.

Several banks and other businesses promptly trotted off up Central to raise new offices, the idea being that the rest of the corridor between them and downtown would soon fill up with soaring high-rises. Obviously, it never quite happened, and between 1972, when Reichert came to work for the city, and 1985, when a new general plan was adopted, enthusiasm from the Washington-to-Camelback, Seventh-to-Seventh idea waned.

Today, the official vision of downtown is narrowed to First Avenue to First Street and north to Camelback.

A number of factors dimmed the original vision, Reichert said. For one thing, the air pollution and traffic problems came to be bad enough as they were. Jamming thousands more people and cars into acres and acres of high rises would have strangled us.

For another thing, new technologies, new economies and new corporate structures meant companies didn't need huge high-rises to hold everybody they needed to do the job. A midrise building now may do where a 30-story high-rise was called for before.

CLASS NOTES: A number of you dispute last week's report on the question of whether one's hair grows faster in warm weather, despite the fact that an eminent dermatologist says that idea is wrong. Our research budget, devoted as it is almost entirely to lunch, does not allow for any independent scientific research on this question. We do, however, remain open to further proof, one way or another.

Are You Kidding? These Are Jokes?

March 26, 2000

A recent column on the troubling shortage of weather jokes brought quite a response, and I must say some you should be ashamed of yourselves. I hope you're not kissing your children with those mouths.

Actually, the one about the lawyer and the St. Bernard was pretty good, but in the interest of what passes for good taste here at *The Republic*, I won't be printing it.

And the Ole and Lena joke was a mistake, even if it was weather-related. I am now awash in Ole and Lena jokes, very few of which have anything to do with the weather and most of which are astoundingly vulgar.

This is one of the few I could print and still keep my job:

Ole and Lena are in bed one night when the phone rings. Ole picks it up, listens a moment and yells, "How would I know? Do you think I'm a weatherman?" and slams the receiver down.

"Who was that?" Lena asks.

"I don't know," Ole says. "Some guy who wanted to know if the coast was clear."

I didn't say it was good. I just said it wasn't dirty.

Here's one I got by e-mail from a woman named Leah Sapir, who, if it is the Leah Sapir I think it is, is a real nice lady who used to live across the street from me. How many Leah Sapirs could there be?

Anyway, here it is:

John and Mary live right on the Arizona-California line with the Colorado River running right along the western edge of their property.

One winter there's a huge rainstorm. It rains for days and days, and when it finally stops, John goes outside and sees the flood has changed the course of the river and it now runs on the eastern edge of their land.

John is amazed. He runs into the house and yells, "Mary! Guess what? We're not in Arizona anymore. We're in California."

"Thank goodness," Mary replies. "I don't think I could take another one of those Arizona summers."

Come on. That wasn't bad. It's better than this one:

A tourist stops for gas out in the middle of the Arizona desert and strikes up a conversation with the grizzled old man who runs the station.

"Does it ever rain around here?" the tourist asks, eying the endless expanse of sand and cactus.

"Do you know the story from the Bible of how it once rained for 40 days and 40 nights?" the old-timer asks.

"Sure, everyone knows that," the tourist answers.

The old man says: "Well, we got about a quarter inch."

Get it? Forty days, 40 nights, quarter of an inch? Maybe it's better spoken than written.

OK, try this:

A cowboy boards a train in Yuma and joins a card game with three traveling salesmen as the train crosses the Arizona desert. A bottle is produced and the cowboy generously offers to provide ice for their drinks. He disappears to the baggage car and returns with ice.

As the trip wears on, he brings out more ice. Finally, one of the salesmen asks for more ice, but the cowboy declines. "If I use any more," he said, "the body won't keep 'til Phoenix."

A Desert? Hah! It's A Jungle Out There

April 2, 2000

It's time to open the mailbag and pretend I know the answer to your outdoor recreation/weather questions. And today's question is especially important because it involves animals that could kill you and not even think twice about it.

Actually, I doubt that many animals think twice about anything. I have a parakeet, and as far as I can tell, it has never even thought once about anything. Certainly not about killing me.

Anyway, the question: *Since we moved to Arizona, my daughter and I have become avid hikers. The other day we saw our first rattlesnake. How many kinds of rattlesnakes are there around here?*

Answer: I hate to tell you this, but there are a lot of them. And not just rattlesnakes. There are coral snakes, and a lot of others, including Gila monsters and killer bees. We're not supposed to call them killer bees anymore. Africanized bees is the term. Call 'em what you like, they're not nice neighbors.

The good news is your chances of being bitten or stung or otherwise killed by any of these creatures are fairly small, unless you're a dope or just naturally unlucky. A study a few years ago showed, as I recall, that the primary victims of rattlesnake bites are young, White males who had been drinking. Of course, the primary cause of a lot of problems is young, White males who have been drinking.

Snakes: There are 11 species of rattlesnakes in Arizona and, for the most part, they are best left alone. Technically, they are pit vipers, which have triangular heads, large fangs and pupils that resemble vertical slits. Much like some editors I've had.

It's not surprising that you saw a rattler recently. They emerge for the season in March and April. During the summer, they are more active at night.

If you're hiking or climbing, don't put your hands where you can't see. Rattlers, affectionately known as buzz worms, don't always rattle before they strike, and yes, baby snakes can be venomous.

You don't even want to know about coral snakes. They don't have fangs and they don't have slitty eyes and instead of injecting venom in one quick shot, they chew on you for a while. Gross.

Coral snakes have black snouts and red, yellow and black rings. Other, harmless snakes have similar colors, but their snouts aren't black and the red and yellow bands don't touch. If the red and yellow bands touch and it just chewed on you, man, you're fried. Get some help right away. Don't call me to tell me to say you hate the Phoenix temperature range chart and, oh, by the way, you just got chewed on by a coral snake. Get to a doctor.

Gila monsters: I actually saw a Gila monster once at Squaw Peak Park. Some young, White males who had been drinking were throwing rocks at it.

Gila monsters are the largest U.S. lizard, up to 22 inches, and the only venomous U.S. lizard. They're shy, slow-moving things and would be quite happy if you didn't stop and say, "Hey, there's one of them Gila monsters. Watch me swing it by its tail."

Legend has it that Gila monster venom is especially toxic because the lizard does not have an anus and secretes waste through its mouth. (I hope you're not reading this over breakfast.) This isn't true, but its venom is considered to be at least as toxic as that of most rattlesnakes, and if you did manage to tick one off to the point that it chewed on you, you should get some help right away.

There's more — scorpions and black widows and brown recluse spiders. My advice would be to either stay home, which wouldn't be much fun; take care and use common sense; or keep a young, White male who has been drinking with you at all times and let him get chewed on.

Opaque Questions Cloud The Issue

April 6, 2000

Here's a question I get asked a lot:

OK, not a lot, really, but it's a question that came in twice from two people in the space of a week or so, which kind of makes it a lot.

Actually, I do get asked certain questions a lot, but they tend to run along lines of inquiry I probably shouldn't go into here. Stuff like:

"Is this the lady of the house?"

or:

"Could you possibly be any dumber?"

or:

"Did you get dressed in the dark this morning?"

or:

"What were you thinking?"

or:

"Are you new here?"

or:

"What's wrong with your hair?"

or:

"Is that it?"

Anyway, this is the question I received twice this past week or so:

What is the difference between partly cloudy and partly sunny?

What a question! Could you possibly be any dumber? Did you think of this question while you were getting dressed in the dark? What were you thinking? Is that it?

Sorry, just venting a bit there.

Actually, this is a very good question and one that I never really thought about much, but which now intrigues me greatly, especially because it came in twice in a week.

My first guess would have been that there's not much difference at all, kind of like the difference between the two major political parties or the difference between Madonna's cover of "American Pie" and a that crud under the refrigerator.

You know, there should be some sort of law about stuff like that. But I digress.

It turns out there actually is a difference between partly cloudy and partly sunny, according to Austin Jamison, a meteorologist at the Phoenix office of the National Weather Service and a very patient person who is willing to speak slowly and in words of few syllables for those of us who don't catch on very quickly.

First of all, says he: It is a somewhat subjective matter. But in a nutshell, if there is going to be less than half opaque cloud cover, the forecast will be partly sunny. If there is going to be more than half opaque cloud cover, it will be partly cloudy.

There also is a day/night issue here. The degree of daytime cloud cover tends to affect, obviously, the partly sunny question because a partly sunny forecast for the night hours would be fairly remarkable and perhaps the subject of an entire column.

Opaque is one of those words that has always given me trouble (see question No. 2 above). I always have to look it up. In the case of cloudiness, it means you can't really see the blue sky very well or the stars or very much moonlight.

If you have any more weather questions, send them along. Again, see question No. 2 above. Maybe all the others, too.

2 Ideas On Bend In 7th Avenue
April 16, 2000

We blush to admit that this week's questions were so hard that we spent the better part of the week looking out the windows, admiring the view from the lofty new headquarters of Valley 101 and training the Valley 101 research lab's sophisticated telescope on various items of intellectual interest. Some of you people really should keep your shades drawn.

This week we have not one, but two questions, lumped together here because they are both streets-related:

First Q: *Why does Seventh Avenue curve between Indian School and Camelback roads, when all the other major streets in the area run straight?*

Second Q: *What is the origin of the name Tatum, as in Tatum Boulevard?*

Both these matters proved to be much more difficult to answer than we expected, and mild panic set in late in the week as pesky deadlines loomed. Hence, we have come to regret spending so much time conducting extensive research with the aforementioned telescope.

Fortunately, as the hour grew late, we discovered our new best friend: John Jacquemart, historian, Realtor and a member of the Phoenix Historic Preservation Commission. He's brilliant. He knows everything. At this very moment, highly trained technicians from the Valley 101 Communications Division are busy installing high-speed fiber optical digital microwave VHF satellite ATM G-9 cables, or something like that, to Mr. Jacquemart's home, office, automobile and good blue suit so that we might be in instant communication with him at any time day or night when stumped by difficult questions, as opposed to having to do any actual work looking up answers ourselves.

First A: We got some varying responses to this one. Mostly this: That when the Phoenix town site was surveyed in the late 1800s, the surveyor made a mistake, deviated from true north, and hence the curve.

The problem with this is that, when the town site was laid out in the late 1800s, the northern limit was something like Van Buren or Roosevelt streets. As late as 1948, Phoenix's northern boundary was Indian School Road and everything north of that was Maricopa County. So we can't even be sure the original survey of Seventh Avenue went that far north.

Jacquemart's answer: "The legend is that the street workers, when they took lunch, imbibed and when they went back to work they weren't going straight."

Legend? Maybe, maybe not, but it works for us, having, as they say, been there, done that and acquired the T-shirts, mostly stained.

One way or another, inept surveyor or loopy street workers, Seventh Avenue curves not by design but by error. At least it breaks the monotony.

Second A: This one stumped the best and the brightest at both Phoenix City Hall and Paradise Valley Town Hall, although we must report they all tried very hard, and the lady who answers the phone in Paradise Valley is really sweet. She should get a big raise.

Jacquemart's answer: Russ Tatum. By golly, this guy is smart.

Russ Tatum, who died in the late 1930s, was an early developer of the area, a landowner, a member of the Paradise Valley Water Commission and a visionary with plans for that part of the Valley.

Real Rash Of Heat Hasn't Arrived Yet

April 29, 2000

I have been asked, now that it has hit 100 for the first time this year, to discuss butt rash.

I am reluctant to take up this topic, at least right now, because only wimps and newcomers think 100 degrees is hot. Everyone else knows the worst of it — that the peak of the butt rash season is yet to come, and that this week's flirtation with 100 was only a peck on the cheek compared to what Nature will inflict on us over the next few months.

Nonetheless, in the interest of public health and in the interest of seeing if I can get the words "butt rash" in the paper, I have decided to pursue the matter.

Butt rash is a red, prickly affliction of one's buttocks brought on by hot weather. It's also fun to say.

Primary victims are people with vinyl seats in their vehicles, people with no or ineffective air-conditioning at home or in their vehicles and people who wear a lot of synthetic fibers, especially across the caboose.

Talcum powder might help, but the reporter in the next cubicle thinks it gives you cancer. She said you should put ice in your pants. I would recommend a soothing, non-staining lotion or salve.

In cases of severe butt rash, see your physician. Or your auto reupholsterer.

Prickly Pear Fruit Makes Candy, Jelly

April 30, 2000

Q: *Are cactus candy and cactus jelly really made out of cactus?*

A: There was a time when we would have brought several samples of cactus candy and jelly back for testing in the Valley 101 Research Laboratory. But with the recent shrinking of the paper, we had to pack up lab equipment and put it in storage. It was either that or the bowling trophies.

So, in the absence of a detailed scientific analysis, we put all our trust in Amelio Cassiato, manager of the Cactus Candy Co. in central Phoenix, which, by the way, has a really cool cactus sign out in front. The company, at 3010 N. 24th St., has been in business since 1942, so one can assume its manager knows whereof he speaks.

Yes, indeed, said he, cactus candy and cactus jelly really are made out of cactus.

Specifically, they are made out of the fruit of the prickly pear cactus, which the company buys by the barrel from a cactus distributor.

With the prickly pear fruit in hand, you make cactus candy or jelly the same way you would make, say, apple candy or jelly, except, as Cassiato notes, if you're careless in handling prickly pear fruit "you remember it for a while."

Prickly pears are interesting in that they produce both the fruit and a vegetable — the cactus pads, known as nopales.

Native Americans used nopales as food, as a dressing for wounds or bruises, and even crushed them to use the sticky juice in mortar or whitewash.

As a vegetable, nopales are said to taste like green beans or asparagus, and can be grilled or used in salads, casseroles, soups or other dishes.

They have no cholesterol, no saturated fat and only 60 calories per cup, so they are good for you, provided you remember to take the spines off before you eat them.

A Q To Keep Us On Our Toes
May 14, 2000

Here at Valley 101 headquarters, white-coated lab technicians have been working round-the-clock to answer one of the greatest questions ever to cross the Valley 101 transom:

Do your feet get bigger when you move to the desert?

You know, we spent hours flipping pancakes, doing day labor, weeding soybeans to get through college, followed by years of crawling over the broken reputations of colleagues and competitors to arrive at a place of relative safety in journalism, and it comes to this: Do your feet get bigger when you move to the desert?

But we digress.

Hours of research, misinterpreted by some of our less-polished masters as watching Cubs games, failed to produce a firm scientific yes or no.

However, anecdotal evidence from readers, some of whom surely have an extra chromosome, has flooded in. A common theory: sandals.

For example, this from a reader who claims to be "M. Hamilton":

"Since I moved here three years ago, my feet have grown a half shoe size. Some of my friends have suggested that it's because people here tend to wear sandals, which spreads out your feet."

Class: Do you people actually sit around the Valley 101 student union discussing your feet? "Speaking of campaign finance reform, my feet are getting huge."

Reader David Valentine offers this idea:

"It is the natural job of feet to sweat. Due to the lack of humidity in this region, feet are prevented from doing their normal job. (This) causes the subcutaneous tissue to swell, therefore expanding the cutaneous tissue resulting in an expansion of the foot."

Okey-dokey.

Next: Does working for a newspaper make your brain smaller?

Roof Rocks Help Cool Hot House
May 28, 2000

Q: *Recently, I saw a house in Tempe that had large rocks on the roof. I mentioned this to a friend who had grown up here, and he said it used to be quite common, but he didn't know why. Can you help?*

A: Of course, sir. Help is our middle name.

Which is not to say we actually had ever heard of such a thing and, we blush to admit, when we first read your question we decided you perhaps had ingested some controlled substance. We felt much the same way early one recent morning when we groggily caught a glimpse of the haircut we had gotten the previous evening and, for an instant, wondered whether we had been eating peyote before telling the barber to cut it real short. We had not.

But we digress.

Rocks on the roof? Who to call but the estimable Max Underwood, professor of architecture at Arizona State University, a specialist in Valley architecture, and hail-fellow-well-met.

Underwood says your native friend is correct. Rocks on the roof can be traced to the Native Americans who lived here long before anyone dreamed of professional hockey and were adopted by homesteaders.

The idea is thus: During the day the rocks soak up the sun's heat. In the cool of the night the rocks give off the heat and because hot air rises, the escaping heat would cause a kind of updraft that would help cool off the house.

There still are a few older houses around town, said Underwood, with good-sized rocks on their roofs, notably the Mitchell Park area of Tempe.

And a colleague tells us she recently saw a new house, near 56th Street and Shea Boulevard, that had adapted this ancient technology.

We would have gone by to see it, but we were too occupied looking for a lawyer willing to bring suit for wrongful barbering.

Cool, Clear Sun Tea Is A Safe Drink

June 18, 2000

Q: *As a refugee from the cloudy Northwest, I have been introduced to pleasures of sun tea. But a co-worker says I am just setting a jar of germs out in the sun to incubate. Is sun tea safe?*

A: Thank you for your inquiry. Immediately upon its receipt, we here at the research lab at Valley 101 immediately spit out a mouthful of sun tea, a la Danny Thomas, and went home to lie down with a cool cloth over our chiseled brows to await the onset of food poisoning.

Fortunately, no such malady ensued and, refreshed by the quiet time, we hied ourselves to the telephone and, for a record second straight week, sought the counsel of Susie Lyons of the University of Arizona's Cooperative Extension office.

To her credit, Ms. Lyons did not sigh deeply and dispatched her usual exceedingly helpful advice.

Brewing sun tea is simplicity itself. You stick some tea bags in a glass jar, put a lid on it and leave it out in the sun to brew. Then you bring it inside and exhaust the household's entire supply of ice cubes to cool it to the point that it's drinkable. Que refresente!

Here's the problem, according to Lyons: If the jar is not truly clean, or if you leave the brew in the sun too long, or if you use too many tea bags, or if you're just unlucky, your sun tea can become "thick, ropy or slimy."

If you were to drink thick, ropy or slimy tea, you would be a dope, and you probably would develop flulike symptoms and spend considerable time, as we once heard it described, "talking to Ralph on the big white phone."

And don't, whatever you do, try to pre-sweeten the tea by adding sugar while it brews in the sun. This is inviting trouble of a thick, ropy or slimy nature.

Frying, No Flying, In High Heat
June 21, 2000

One of my masters wants me to fry an egg on the sidewalk. He thinks we should video it and put it up on the Web.

I don't know. I figure if it's hot enough for a sidewalk egg fry, it's too hot to be standing around outside frying eggs.

I told him it was a good idea, but maybe we should wait until it cooled off. Then, I gave him my ballpoint pen and showed him how it works and he went away happy.

I think the last time we did the egg-frying thing was in 1990, when it hit 122 on June 26. It was so hot that some big jets were grounded at Sky Harbor International Airport.

This is why, according to Arv Schultz, a retired commercial pilot and publisher of *Arizona Airways* and the *Sky Harbor Airport News*: At the time, the calculations in the operating manuals for some jets didn't take into account temperatures over 120 degrees.

The temperature has to do with something called "density altitude," which has to do with how much fuel and other weight you can carry and how much runway you need to take off.

"I'm not going to say the air is thinner (when it's hot)," Schultz said. "It's just that the density of the air is such that it requires a long take-off roll."

Steve Biggs, Phoenix's deputy aviation director for operations, said the numbers problem affected Boeing 737s. Other planes, such as DC-9s, had manuals that went over 120.

However, because of the density altitude thing, DC-9s that normally carried 110 passengers were taking off with just 49 people and no luggage on board.

Quakes Not Here, But Just A Shake Away

July 8, 2000

As if I didn't have enough things that terrify me, this turned up in the e-mail this week:

What is the annual frequency of damaging earthquakes in Arizona?

The answer, as is the case with so much of my life, is "I don't know." We do have earthquakes in Arizona, but I do not know the precise frequency of damaging earthquakes. Let's put it this way: Earthquakes in Arizona are like editors with good ideas. Sure, it happens every now and again, and it's surprising when it does, but nothing much ever comes of it.

This is not to say earthquakes are not serious business. There is an Arizona Council for Earthquake Safety that works on building codes and response plans and other such earthquake stuff just in case the Big One does happen.

The earthquakes we do have tend to occur in the far southwestern corner of the state, the tail end of California's San Andreas Fault, and in the area between Flagstaff and the Grand Canyon. There also are some volcanoes up around there, dormant, of course, but you never know. A volcano — that would be something, wouldn't it?

In 1906 and 1912, there were big earthquakes — probably around 6.2 on the Richter scale — just north of Flagstaff. The biggest earthquake (that we know of) in the region was a 7.4 event in 1887 in Mexico about 50 miles southeast of Douglas. It caused damage in Tucson.

Just a couple of months ago, there were a bunch of earthquakes in northern Arizona. A bunch of earthquakes is called a "swarm." "Swarm" is a creepy word. Killer bees swarm. I bet elves swarm. How would you like to run into a swarm of elves?

Anyway, on May 3, there was a 3.2 earthquake in the Painted Desert about 15 miles southwest of Tuba City. The day before, there was a 2.6 earthquake on the North Rim of the Grand Canyon.

Since there really isn't much around those spots to damage, there were no reports of damage.

I could list others, but I have to go to a meeting. One of the editors just had an idea.

Please Step Away From the Window

August 2, 2000

Today's question: *I am terrified of thunderstorms, but my husband loves them. He insists on standing at the window to watch storms. I keep telling him he's going to get hit by lightning, but he says the glass protects him. We have been arguing about this for 36 years.*

Your husband must be rich or good looking, lady, because you certainly can't love him for his brains. Standing in front of a window during a big windy storm, lightning and all, is a crummy idea.

The chances that a lightning bolt would come through the glass and smite your beloved are very slim, but it has been known to happen.

Weather-whiz Randy Cerveny of Arizona State University has pictures of holes that lightning has cut in windows with the precision of a glasscutter.

True, glass is not a particularly good conductor of electricity. The biggest danger in standing by a window during a storm is that the glass would be shattered by the wind, by flying debris or by a lightning strike very close by. This would make something of a mess out of your husband.

You should also avoid the tub or shower during a lightning storm and stay off the phone. Cordless phones are OK.

The real question is, after 36 years, what will you find to argue about now?

What's That After-Rain Aroma?

September 3, 2000

Q: *What exactly causes that fresh/earthy scent when it rains in the Valley? It's a real distinct scent, not flowery or sweet, but more like a fresh, clean smell.*

A: Your question worked its way to the top of the pile at just the right time — Tuesday, when we had that delightful morning rain.

As soon as the skies cleared we leapt into the Valley 101 mobile research lab, and set out to find the source of the scent.

You are right. There was a truly remarkable aroma in the air, which we soon traced to a half-eaten Big Mac under the floor mats in the backseat of the Valley 101 mobile research lab. While we would not describe this as "fresh/earthy" it was definitely distinctive.

After a stop at the car wash, we sought advice from the estimable Carolyn O'Malley, executive director of the Desert Botanical Gardens and an honorary member of the Valley 101 faculty.

Said she: "It's the creosote bush. It's a native and it's all over the Valley. It is very pungent."

And it smells wonderful after a rain.

In fact, O'Malley knows of a couple who had a sprinkler system installed specifically to rain upon their creosote bushes on evenings when they entertain so their guests could enjoy the aroma.

Creosote bushes are members of the evergreen family and are named for the tar-like aroma of their resin.

An interesting thing about creosote bushes: The crown of the plant splits into lobes, which bend over into the soil and send out their own roots and branches, making them clones of the original.

One group of creosote clones found in the Mojave Desert is believed to be about 11,700 years old, perhaps the oldest living plant life we know of.

Colorful Flowers Belie Nasty Plant

September 17, 2000

Q: *Why is it against the law to grow morning glories in Arizona?*

A: It is? Uh-oh. Excuse us. We have to dash home for a few minutes.

Yes, indeed, it is against Arizona law to grow morning glories. As far as we know, no one has ever been sent up for this offense, nor have there ever been, that we are aware of, turf struggles between elements of the criminal underclass vying to control the morning glory trade.

Nonetheless, it turns out that beneath its happy, colorful flowers beat the roots of a really nasty plant.

According to Ed Northam, noxious-weed manager for the state Department of Agriculture, morning glories are "very aggressive, very invasive and very competitive." In this, they remind us of our masters.

Turned loose in a field of cotton or some other crop, morning glories "can get so dense and thick that it can be very difficult or even impossible to harvest the crop," Northam said. They can turn into a "tangled mass of hundreds and hundreds of vines in a square yard."

There are a few native species of morning glory that are legal to grow in Arizona, but Northam said if you see a packet of morning glory seeds in a store or nursery, chances are pretty good that they are a banned variety. Inspectors are always checking for this and other banned plants, but some are bound to get through.

If his crews do find a patch of morning glories, Northam said, they work with the landowner to have them removed. If necessary, the state can have the growth killed off and bill the landowner for the work.

You can find a list of about 50 plants the state considers noxious at www.agriculture.state.az.us.

Keeping Your Cool Amid This Heat

September 24, 2000

Q: *My friend turns his air-conditioning off when he goes to work, goes on vacation or plans on being out of the house for more than a few hours. It gets up to 100 degrees in his house. Is he really saving money on his electric bill?*

A: Coincidentally, as this is written, the air-conditioning is off here at the Valley 101 offices on the No. 9 parapet of the Dark Tower. Our masters, who are sipping cool drinks and being fanned and fed grapes by interns, tell us this is a temporary malfunction, but in some of the more primitive areas of the newsroom there are mutterings of human experiments being carried out.

Nonetheless, brow dripping, we soldier on.

We have reason to believe that your friend — and we don't mean to get too technical here — is a dope. We got partial confirmation of this by consulting with the estimable Scott Harelson, a Salt River Project spokesman.

Yes, said Harelson, if you are going to be gone for a long time, like a couple weeks or so, you might save money and energy by turning the air-conditioner off. However, the unit is going to have to work really, really hard to cool the place off when you get home, because the whole house — walls, floors, furniture, pots and pans and the goldfish — are going to be pretty well baked by then. So your savings might be questionable.

But if you're only going to work or going to be out for a little while, SRP recommends turning the thermostat up just 4 to 6 degrees above your comfort level. Turning the air-conditioning off for a short-term outing will not save money or energy because of the effort involved in cooling the house down.

Our masters insist the air-conditioning will be on again soon. Meanwhile, they have called for more grapes.

Meaning Of KTAR Is Clear
October 15, 2000

Q: *Is it true that the call letters of radio station KTAR stand for Keep Taking the Arizona Republic?*

A: We receive two types of questions here at Valley 101 — good questions and less-than-good questions. The difference is this: Good questions require little, if any, actual work on our part to answer. Less-than-good questions require that we tear ourselves away from more pressing duties — drinking coffee, gossiping, having lunch — and do some actual work.

With some regret, we must tell you, sir, that your question, while interesting, fell into the less-than-good category, and, sighing deeply, we set aside the crossword and delved into the dusty Valley 101 archives to find the answer.

That answer was lodged deep in the bowels of *All the Time a Newspaper*, an excellent history of this newspaper by former *Republic* reporter Earl Zarbin. And the answer is, yes, indeed. KTAR, which went on the air in 1922, was owned for some time by the Arizona Publishing Co. which owned the *Arizona Republican*, which became *The Arizona Republic* in 1929.

Actually, the newspaper shared ownership of the radio station with the Electrical Equipment Co. of Phoenix, which had opened and operated another station, KFAD. We do not know what KFAD's call letters stood for, if anything, but indeed KTAR stood for Keep Taking the *Arizona Republic*, which we feel is a noble sentiment even today.

In The Dark On Valley's Sunshine

October 20, 2000

Today's question: *Have we ever had a day in the Valley of the Sun when the sun did not shine?*

This is weather-wonkism at its finest, don't you think? Arcane, obscure, of no practical use that I can think of. You know, sometimes I feel a little guilty about encouraging this sort of stuff.

It is a pertinent question in the sense that, depending on which list you look at, Phoenix is often considered to be the sunniest city in the country, and perhaps even the world.

Of course, technically speaking, there could never be a day without sunshine. If there were we would all be lost in gloom as dark as my masters' hearts. The National Weather Service does, however, take daily sunshine readings based on the percentage of the possible sunshine for the day. This is determined by the number of minutes between sunrise and sunset during which sunlight casts a shadow on a sensor. If, for instance, there are 720 minutes between sun-up and sun-down and the sensor reads a shadow during 648 of those minutes, we had 90 percent of possible sunshine.

OK so far?

This year to date we have had only one day with zero percent of possible sunshine — March 6.

The annual average of possible sunshine in Phoenix is a well-lit 85 percent. By comparison, Seattle's average is 46 percent.

December is the most dimly lit month of the year for the Valley with an average of 77 percent of possible sunshine. The gloomiest month ever in Phoenix was December 1914 when our forefathers and foremothers enjoyed just 47 percent of the sunshine they were due.

The Valley's longest streak of sunny days was June 12 to July 9, 1928 — 28 days of 100 percent sunshine. The longest dark spell was Nov. 22-24, 1965 — three days of 0 percent.

Legend City A Failure In Its Own Era

October 22, 2000

Q: *What is Legend City?*

A: Gee whiz, Legend City. We had forgotten all about Legend City.

For better or for worse, it is not "What is Legend City?" but "What was Legend City?" That 58-acre chapter in the Valley's pop-culture history closed in 1983, but there remains a certain age group of Valley residents who hold its memory in fond regard.

Legend City was an amusement park that stood near 56th and Washington streets. Actually, it was originally planned more as a Wild West theme park than an amusement park by investors who dreamed of a Disneyland on the desert.

There was a steam locomotive running on a 1-mile track, an Indian village, a ghost town, a Mexican village, miniature golf, a roller coaster and other rides.

In some of its later reincarnations, it was also a concert venue. Compton Terrace was first located at Legend City.

Alas, the theme-park idea was not a particularly good one. The site was not large enough to be truly big-time, and Valley residents spoiled by Disneyland found Legend City lacking. Plus, crowds dwindled in the summer months when the idea of hauling the kiddies from ride to ride in 110-degree temperatures was not all that appealing.

In its first seven months, Legend City, developed at a cost of $5 million, lost more than $150,000. By the end of 1964, management couldn't afford to print a financial statement for shareholders.

A series of optimistic management changes followed over the years and the park staggered on until 1983 when it closed for good.

The site was purchased by the Salt River Project, which tore down the whole shebang and opened its headquarters there in 1991.

After Last Summer, Why Am I So Cold Now

November 12, 2000

Q: *I just survived my first Arizona summer and now I'm freezing. Why am I so cold in what was shirt-sleeve weather in Wisconsin?*

A: An excellent question, madam, and very much the mirror image of a hot-weather question we seem to recall having discussed in an earlier Valley 101 class.

We feel your pain. When we first arrived in Arizona, lo these many Novembers ago, we marveled on many winter mornings, as we drove to work in shirt-sleeves and with the car windows rolled down, at the many people we saw bundled in overcoats, boots and gloves.

Nowadays, in much the same weather as those first November mornings, we shiver and draw the tattered afghan closer over our bony shoulders and throw another *Republic* employees-conduct manual on the fire.

No, it is not a matter, as people so often say, of your blood thinning out.

When you live in extreme heat, an Arizona summer, for example, your body adapts to the conditions in many ways, including something called vasodilation.

This is a process in which your blood vessels expand and move closer to the surface of your skin to help keep you cooler. All this is accomplished without your bidding.

When the weather suddenly switches from really hot to cool, it takes time for your body to readjust and de-vasodilate, if there is such a word. Hence, while at home in Wisconsin you may have found a high of 60 almost balmy, in the Valley you are shivering. In fact, on one recent afternoon with the temperature in the high 50s, we found ourselves in the company of a longtime Valley resident whose teeth were literally chattering from the cold. It was kind of cute.

Dry Canal? Just Taking Out The Trash

December 3, 2000

Q: *What happened to the canals? The water is gone and there's just trash in there.*

A: The water's gone? Oh, my God, this is it. Grab your most precious belongings and flee!

Ha! Just kidding. Just another example of that puckish humor we like to indulge in here at the shabby but genteel headquarters of Valley 101.

You obviously live south of the Salt River, because on Nov. 24 the Salt River Project began its annual cleanup of canals south of the Salt. Canals north of the river will be drained and cleaned starting January 5.

Every winter, when demand for irrigation water is low, SRP crews drain the canals for maintenance and general cleanup.

You don't even want to think about what they find in there. Imagine the back of your refrigerator multiplied by 131 miles of canals.

Thom Bawden, SRP groundwater superintendent, said that in addition to the usual run-of-the-mill litter, crews have found guns, safes, construction junk, lots of shopping carts and even cars. One year they found a Corvette.

Bawden said the interesting stuff — guns, safes, cars, etc. — is turned over to the police. Everything else goes to the dump, although last year SRP gave some of it to some Scottsdale high school students, who used it to make some sculptures, which were very nice, providing you like sculptures made out of canal junk.

Do not worry your pretty little heads over the canal fish. To keep down aquatic weeds, SRP uses white amurs, which, like my masters, are bottom-feeders. Since, unlike my masters, they serve a useful function, the fish are herded to safety by amur-herders as the canals are dried up.

Will New Master Be Wonkish?

December 8, 2000

As you may know, I have a new master. A new thane walks the halls of the Dark Tower.

I haven't met him yet, but I have nonetheless been busy practicing knuckling my forelock. Since I don't have a forelock, I now have a small bruise on my forehead, but I think it's worth it.

I should also be brushing up on fawning, but instead I am busy answering questions like this:

Has there ever been a day when the difference between Arizona's high and low temperatures was 100 degrees or more?

Sometimes I think there is a cabal of weather wonks out there who meet once a month or so to think up the most arcane weather questions they can and then e-mail them to me under fictitious names. This one came from someone who claims his name is "Gary." Sounds made up to me.

There are a couple of problems here. One is that I can't find anyone who keeps track of something that odd. The second is that I don't even know if this new guy cares about weather or the such. What if he's interested in mineralogy or cows or something? Geez.

Anyway, the place to start seems to be with the extremes. The hottest day ever in Arizona was June 29, 1994, when it hit 128 at Lake Havasu City. That day the low in Flagstaff was 42, a gap of 86 degrees, and it seems likely that it probably wasn't too much cooler anyplace else.

The coldest reading ever in the state was 40-below on January 7, 1971, at Hawley Lake. The high that day in Phoenix was 46, and in Yuma it was 49.

So, the answer to the question is: Probably not. However, here's a little wonk treat for you: On January 20, 1971, just 13 days after the record low, the high at Hawley Lake was 63. That is believed to be the greatest temperature range in a single calendar month for an Arizona reporting station.

Mailbox Stones Hex Dirty Birds
December 10, 2000

Q: *We recently moved here from Pittsburgh, and we have an extremely important question about Sun City West: Why do residents put stones on their mailboxes?*

A: We have heard of stones on roofs and stones on lawns, but we have to admit that stones on mailboxes was a new one to us. Of course, here at Valley 101, almost anything is a new one to us.

We considered examining this phenomenon firsthand, but the Valley 101 mobile research lab was in the shop, so we set hand to telephone and called the Sun City West Visitors and Information Center, reasoning that we were, in a sense, visiting and in need of some information.

And we quickly had an answer, thanks to the exceedingly helpful Kay Johns, who works there.

This is why, according to Ms. Johns, people in Sun City West put rocks on their mailboxes:

"To keep the birds off."

Apparently, the theory is that if you create an uneven surface on your mailbox, it keeps birds from landing there and pooping thereupon. And there is general agreement, at least in Sun City West, that birds pooping on your mailbox is not a good thing.

Ms. Johns herself does not have rocks on her mailbox, but she did volunteer that she carries a rubber snake with her whenever she plays golf.

Why, you may well ask, does Ms. Johns carry a rubber snake with her when she plays golf?

For the same reason that people put rocks on their mailboxes.

When she gets out of her golf cart to take another whack, she leaves the rubber snake on the seat to keep birds from landing there and pooping thereupon, which could give all new meaning to the golfing term "birdie."

History Gives 2 Main Cities Differences

January 7, 2001

Q: *My grandpa and grandma live in Tucson, and when we visit them, I always wonder why are Phoenix and Tucson so different?*

A: This is an excellent question. The answer would fill a volume or two, but the short explanation is: History, dear child, it's all about history.

In the great scheme of things, Phoenix is a fairly young city. Granted, the Hohokam and other Native Americans lived around here for centuries, but a permanent European presence was not established until the Army opened Fort McDowell in 1865. The hay camp that supplied the fort eventually became Phoenix.

By contrast, Tucson's European roots go back to 1694, when the tireless missionary Father Kino founded a small mission roughly near the Miracle Mile overpass at Interstate 10. Not far away was another village Kino called San Cosme de Tucson. It was more or less the northernmost point of the Spanish settlement in what is now Arizona.

The site grew to be a Spanish presidio, a fortress against Apache raids and, to make a very long story very short, eventually became good old Tucson, the Old Pueblo.

The name Tucson, by the way, comes from the Pima word schookson, according to historian Marshall Trimble. It means "black at the foot of" and probably refers to the dark base of Sentinel Mountain, also known as "A" Mountain.

It is our considered opinion, young reader, that time has given Tucson a stronger sense of Hispanic culture, architecture and history and a somehow different outlook on matters than you might find in brash, young Phoenix, still a relative newcomer to Arizona.

Sky Harbor Name Dates From 1929

January 14, 2001

Q: *How did Sky Harbor International Airport get its name?*

A: We take up this question with some reluctance because the entire staff and faculty of Valley 101 has a deep abhorrence of airports, which extends to even writing about them. At the same time, however, we always thought Sky Harbor was a cool name, in a 1950-ish, let's-go-out-to-the-airport-and-watch-the-planes-land kind of way.

Actually, the name Sky Harbor goes back to 1929, a fact we found in *Desert Wings*, a history of the airport written by Michael Jones, a city Aviation Department employee.

According to Jones, Sky Harbor was named by J. Parker Van Zant, the owner of Scenic Airlines, who came here in 1928 looking for a Phoenix base for his company, "The Rainbow Route Across the Grand Canyon."

There already were three airports in Phoenix, but Van Zant wanted his own place, so he bought 278 acres of cotton fields east of 24th Street and south of the Southern Pacific railroad tracks and turned it into a landing field.

According to Jones: "By February of 1929, the airport was officially titled Phoenix Sky Harbor Airport. Whether the name came from a desire by Scenic to name all its airports Sky Harbor or by the idea of a "harbor" for aircraft, no one knows for sure."

Scenic went broke later that year and sold the airport to a group of local investors, the Acme Investment Co.

In 1934, Acme leased the airport to Maricopa County, but the county backed out of the deal a year later. Acme pushed the city to buy the airport, and the city resisted until American Airlines, which had been using Sky Harbor since 1930, threatened to cut off passenger and airmail service. The city relented and bought the airport for $100,000 in July 1936.

Intriguing Landmark Lessons
January 21, 2001

Today, class, we take up two questions, both dealing with mountains, both about landmarks that tend to be large and readily noticeable.

Q: *From U.S. 60 near Apache Junction we can see an enormous painting of the word "Phoenix" with an arrow pointing toward the city. This has always intrigued us.*

Q: *Near the top of Shaw Butte is the foundation of what must have been a large building. What was it?*

A: As to the Phoenix sign: The word and the arrow were spelled out with whitewashed rocks in the 1950s by a group of Boy Scouts on the side of a mountain in what is now Maricopa County's Usery Mountain Recreation Area.

The sign was meant as a guide for pilots who might be wandering around looking for Phoenix, which of course was much smaller back then and easier to miss.

Mike Juliano, Usery Mountain park supervisor, said about three years ago his staff organized a group of Scouts to refurbish the sign, but his office had so many complaints about the sign disturbing the natural setting that it is doubtful it will be fixed up again in the future.

For the Shaw Butte question, we turned to the exceedingly helpful Jeff Spellman, a Phoenix parks ranger and Sunnyslope native who knew all about it.

The foundation is all that remains of the Cloud 9 restaurant, which in its day was one of Phoenix's swankiest eateries.

Patrons were shuttled up the rough road to the Cloud 9 in four-wheel-drive vehicles and, as they ate, enjoyed spectacular views of the Valley.

Regrettably, the Cloud 9 burned to the ground early on Nov. 8, 1964, and was never rebuilt. The site later became part of the Phoenix Mountains Preserve system.

Mileage Markers No Mystery
February 4, 2001

Last week, class, you were asked to research the story of a man who used to drive around painting mileage numbers on lids of 5-gallon paint cans and placing them on fences and posts.

We are pleased to report that more than 120 of you have earned gold stars in the Valley 101 Big Book of Life for your diligence in writing or calling with your reports.

The mileage man was one Denny Gleason, who died in 1976. Basically, he believed we needed a new system of numbering things based on mileage coordinates from the center of the Valley. Lots of people said his starting point was Central Avenue and Washington Street.

However, Chip Gleason, the mileage man's great-nephew, said his uncle's zero point was the Gila and Salt River Baseline Meridian, which is the zero point for all land measurements in the state. I think he measured and marked distances from both spots.

"He was a real character," Chip Gleason said, "and he was probably the nicest guy you'd ever want to meet."

Gleason and two brothers owned an exclusive haberdashery in downtown Phoenix, but lost it during the Depression. At some point after that he hit upon his mileage coordinates plan. A marker of 1N, 2W, for example, would mean you were one mile north and two miles west of Gleason's zero-point. He drove all over the area in an old beat-up car posting his markers far and wide.

Gleason also sold travel guides based on his system, and for years lobbied the county Board of Supervisors to adopt it as official.

He also was an accomplished pianist and tickled the ivories in a number of bars and restaurants all over town.

Most of Gleason's signs are long gone. We were directed to one in north-central Phoenix but only with the promise that we would not reveal its location, lest it be swiped.

East, West Won't Meet In Butter Tray

February 11, 2001

Q: *Why are sticks of butter sold here not the same as butter sold in the East? The Arizona kind is shorter and fatter. It doesn't fit on the butter trays I bought years ago in Connecticut.*

A: We have to confess that sometimes, in our darker hours, we sit alone under the light of a single naked bulb here at the shabby but genteel headquarters of Valley 101 and pull a bottle of root beer out of our battered desk and wonder if it's time to give it up. Have all the great questions been asked? All the great mysteries solved? Are there no mountains left to climb?

And then a question like yours arrives, and our faith in the essential oddness of our readers is restored. A new day dawns. Wiping the root beer foam from our lips, we turn our chiseled visage to face a new challenge.

And we learn, yes, indeed, butter is different here. Who knew?

As it turned out, the exceedingly helpful Harold Metzger, sales purchasing manager for the United Dairymen of Arizona, knew.

"It's just a regional preference. In the West, butter comes in a 'Western flat.' In the East it's called an 'Elgin quarter.' There is no real reason for it other than regional preference," said he.

"It's the same reason that in the East people prefer white cheddar cheese, and in the Midwest and West they prefer yellow cheddar cheese. It's just a matter of a little food coloring."

Frankly, the thought of white cheddar cheese makes us a little queasy, but that is neither here nor there.

We are told by a usually reliable butter consumer of our acquaintance that at least one brand of butter sold hereabouts comes in Elgin quarters — Land O'Lakes — but we do not know this for a fact. We will check it out the next time we go to the store for root beer.

Big Counties Make Sense In Arizona

February 18, 2001

Q: *I'm from Indiana, and this is my question: Why are Arizona counties so big?*

A: When we first read your question, we were a bit nonplussed, but this is not too surprising because we here at Valley 101 are rather easily nonplussed. Then we remembered we left our pluss in our other pants, and, reassured, we set about to learn the answer.

First, some history:

After Arizona became a U.S. territory in 1863, four counties were created — Mojave, Pima, Yuma and Yavapai. A fifth county, Pah-Ute, was claimed — and taxed — by both Arizona and Nevada, with Nevada emerging as the winner. Maricopa County was created in 1871, and others came along over time when need arose.

When statehood was won in 1912, the state Constitution allowed for 14 counties, and this was the case until 1983, when La Paz County was carved out of northern Yuma County because people there were tired of driving so far to Yuma to do official business, a plight with which we can sympathize.

Anyway, we do indeed have big counties. Maricopa County, at 9,222 square miles, is bigger than Massachusetts, and Coconino County is almost twice as big as Maricopa.

Look at it this way: Why would we need smaller counties? What or who would they govern? Gila monsters?

Indiana, which has a population density of about 154 people per square mile, has 92 counties. Arizona has something like 35 people per square mile and the aforementioned 15 counties.

With numbers like that, smaller administrative units wouldn't make sense. If we cut Arizona up into 92 counties, we'd end up with a lot of teeny-tiny counties with hardly anyone in them.

Plus, it would be hard to think up all those county names, although if any new counties ever were to be created, we would modestly suggest that Thompsonia would make a dandy name.

Park Statue Dedicated To Progress

February 25, 2001

Q: *At Encanto Park there is a statue of a man with some test tubes. I can't find out much about it. Can you help?*

A: Indeed we can, dear lady. And here at Valley 101, we are especially pleased to help with this one because, with our scholarly bent, we have a fondness for this statue, which is dedicated to "World Progress Through Scientific Research in the Laboratory."

It is near the park's 15th Avenue entrance and shows a man in a lab coat, his sleeves rolled up. In front of him is an array of laboratory flasks and tubing.

The statue was unveiled in 1958, fulfilling the last wishes of one Helen Rogers, who died an elderly widow in 1952 and left the city $1,500 to erect a monument to scientific progress.

Unfortunately, the Chicago sculptor named in the will to do the job wanted $50,000, and the project languished until 1957. By then, interest on the bequest had grown $2,700 and Rogers' trustees and the Phoenix Parks Board commissioned Charles Badger Martin for the job.

Martin, an illustrator for the city by day and a sculptor by night, arrived in Phoenix in 1945 and lived here until his death in 1976.

He fashioned the statue out of lead, brass and copper. But instead of the common method of casting molten metals, he hammered the sheets of metal into the desired shapes.

Other examples of Martin's work include a monument to pioneer women at Wesley Bolin Plaza and a bust of composer and pianist Ignace Paderewski at Arizona State University's Music Library.

We blush bright red to admit that in our reveries, we sometimes wonder if someday a wealthy widow might leave in her will funds for a modest statue of the Valley 101 staff, but if it is all the same to her, we'll take the cash.

Ascending The Heights Of Terror
March 11, 2001

Q: *I'm new to Phoenix, and I love it. I want to see more of the state, but my fear of heights keeps me off steep, winding roads. How can I find out which roads involve cliff-side driving?*

A: We are deeply sympathetic, dear lady. We blush in a manly way to admit it, but such roads sometimes also give us the heebie-jeebies. So do those flying monkeys in *The Wizard of Oz*. Those are really scary.

The simplest answer would be to advise you to stay home. But this would be to deprive yourself of great tracts of Arizona's grandeur. So we feel duty-bound to advise you to steel yourself against your fears. You are, after all, now in Arizona, land of rugged, self-reliant pioneers. You must be brave. Perhaps a driving school or therapist could help.

In the meantime, you'd better stay off U.S. 60 in the Salt River Canyon because it's going to scare the bejabbers out of you. A magnificent, but apparently troubled, great horned owl once committed suicide against our windshield on a stormy night deep in the Salt River Canyon, an experience we found profoundly moving, to say the least.

And until you overcome your fears, you perhaps should also avoid, among other places, the switchbacks at the upper end of Oak Creek Canyon; the drive to the North Rim of the Grand Canyon; the Apache Trail, which goes up to Roosevelt Dam; and U.S. 191 between Clifton and Alpine, which you may be alarmed to learn is sometimes referred to as "The Devil's Highway."

So unless you want to condemn yourself to only driving back and forth from Phoenix to Tucson, you must deal with your fears. And when you do venture out to delight in the glorious scenery you are now missing, be sure to let us know ahead of time. We'll go to Tucson that day.

Want To Know Right Spelling?
Ask Mojaves

March 18, 2001

Q: *Why is Mojave spelled with an "h" in Arizona and with a "j" in California?*

A: It is? By golly, you're right. We never noticed that before. In Arizona, we have Mohave County and the Mohave Mountains and the Mohave Valley and assorted other Mohave things, but in California it's Mojave. Either way, it's pronounced mo-ha-ve, with a long "o" and long "e" and the accent on the second syllable.

Let us start at the beginning: Mohave is an attempt to spell or pronounce the true name of the Native American tribe called the Mojave. It's Pipa Aha Macave, "people who live along the water." Mutavilya, the tribe's spirit-mentor, created the Colorado River and educated the people in civilization. When the Spaniards met them in the 18th century, the Pipa Aha Macave, who are related to the Yuman Indian tribes, were well-to-do farmers who traded with tribes as far away as the Pacific Ocean.

Fort Mojave was established as a military outpost on the east bank of the Colorado in 1859 to protect wagon trains from the Mojaves, who were getting understandably grouchy about the intrusions of migrants and soldiers. The fort was abandoned in 1861 because of the Civil War, reopened in 1863, and in 1890, it was turned over for use as an Indian school.

Today, the Fort Mojave Indian Reservation, based in Needles, covers about 32,000 acres in California, Arizona and Nevada.

According to one of our favorite books, *X Marks the Spot: Historical Names of Places in Arizona*, by Byrd Howell Granger, there have been over the years more than 50 variations in the spelling of Mojave. However, the tribe spells it Mojave and so does the *Arizona Republic* stylebook, and that's good enough for us.

Arizona's use of "h" apparently is an attempt to anglicize the Spanish pronunciation that uses the soft "j," as in Juan or jalapeño.

Don't Fret, Stickers Not Intimidating

March 25, 2001

Q: *I don't understand all the different stickers you see on license plates here.*

A: We have submitted your remark to the Valley 101 research lab for careful analysis, and frankly we are still puzzled.

Is this a question or perhaps just an observation or perhaps even a small, quiet call for help?

We must counsel you not to let this matter bother you. In the great scheme of things, which we recently found on the Web, by the way, license-plate stickers are a small matter. They are certainly not worth the damage they seem to be doing to your self-esteem as you wrestle with this issue. Be assured that the fact that you do not understand them does not in any way make you a lesser person.

You certainly cannot be overly puzzled by the regular stickers that show the effective date of your vehicle registration. If that is what you don't understand, perhaps you are in need of greater help than we can provide.

Perhaps what is bothering you is a small sticker that reads "FLT" that one sometimes spots on license plates. It is an abbreviation for "fleet." There is nothing sinister about this. Last year, the Legislature passed a law that allows people who own two or more vehicles to register them all at the same time. This eliminates the inconvenience of registering one car in, say, February and another in October. These vehicles still are subject to the appropriate emissions-testing rules and all other required fees.

Perhaps you also have seen a car or truck with a "PRM" sticker on the license plate. We doubt that because these stickers are not for cars or trucks. They are for trailers, such as boater trailers or utility trailers. PRM means "permanent registration" and allows the owners of these non-polluting vehicles to register them once for a $75 fee.

Scottsdale's Water Ranch A Costly Goof

April 1, 2001

Q: *We were exploring some back roads in western Arizona when we came to a locked gate with a sign reading, "Planet Ranch, City of Scottsdale." What is Scottsdale doing in La Paz County?*

A: Ah, Planet Ranch. We'd forgotten about that, and there probably are a lot of people in Scottsdale who wish they could forget about it, too. It is one of those "seemed like a good idea at the time" things, the type of thing, we must admit, that checkers the careers of many Valley 101 staff members.

In 1984, Scottsdale paid $11.7 million for the 171,141-acre Planet Ranch in order to gain the rights to water from the Bill Williams River. The idea was to build a pipeline to carry the river water to the Central Arizona Project Canal and thence to Scottsdale.

Scottsdale was not alone in this speculation. Mesa and Phoenix also bought "water farms," and developers were abuzz with plans to buy up tracts of land and peddle the water rights to cities.

However, in a rare burst of cogent thinking, the Legislature realized these schemes could drain rural parts of the state of their water rights. So new laws were passed that sharply limited such enterprises, and the water-ranchers, most notably Scottsdale, were left holding the bag. Not a drop of the Bill Williams ever bedewed Scottsdale.

At the time, the rules required that to retain the water rights, the land had to be farmed, so Scottsdale went into the alfalfa business, with a notable lack of success. In 1993, the city spent $1.18 million on Planet Ranch and earned $626,341 selling alfalfa. This, as they say, is no way to run a railroad.

A few offers to buy the land have come and gone, and changes in the law have lifted the alfalfa bale from Scottsdale's back, but the ranch remains a property of the city of the West's Most Western City.

Mean Caliche Will Punish Green Thumb

April 8, 2001

Q: *Why is the ground so hard here?*

A: Been doing a bit of gardening, have we? Perhaps some landscaping?

You have our deepest sympathy. We feel your blisters, your aching back.

We ourselves, accustomed to the deep loam of our ancestral lands, had never found need to yield a pickaxe until we moved here, lo, those many years ago, and found the ground could only be broken with the help of that pointy tool.

You are correct, the ground is hard here. To test the relative "bounce" of the earth we devised an experiment in which dead weights, in the form of various editors, were to be dropped off the roof of the Valley 101 Research Laboratory, but the subjects of these tests proved to be uncooperative, not to mention surly.

Instead, we turned for an explanation to the elegantly named Simon Peacock, head of the geology department at Arizona State University.

Said he: "Because it is so dry here, clay-rich soil can be quite hard. The summer temperatures are not quite hot enough to bake the clay-rich soil into hard porcelain, but it seems that way.

"Secondly, hard, concrete-like layers called caliche form in desert soils from the salts left behind after groundwater evaporates. Where well-developed, caliche layers can require jack-hammering to get through."

Caliche, in case you are wondering is, pronounced "ca-Lee-chee."

If indeed you are new to the Valley and new to Valley gardening, we would recommend two excellent founts of free wisdom: the University of Arizona's Cooperative Extension Service at (602) 470-8086 and the Desert Botanical Gardens at (480) 941-1217.

Lovebirds Get Wild In The Valley
April 12, 2001

OK, after this question I am declaring a temporary moratorium on bird stuff, especially pigeon stuff.

Some of you are growing increasingly macabre in your suggestions on how to get rid of pigeons. Personally, although I do not like them, I would rather have live pigeons on my roof than rows of dead pigeons impaled on thin, nearly invisible spikes.

So, this is the last bird question for a while:

"I was walking the Red Mountain Ranch area in east Mesa recently when I saw five or six parrot-looking birds with bright green bodies and red heads. What were they?"

My first instinct was to assume you are delusional, which is not necessarily a bad thing, nor would it necessarily distinguish you from many other readers.

But just on the off chance you actually saw these creatures, I called my old buddy, Dr. Robert Witzeman, long a stalwart of the Maricopa Audubon Society, and, by golly, it turns out you saw what you saw.

This is pretty interesting: The birds you saw, Witzeman said, were peach-faced lovebirds — pet birds that either were freed from or escaped from their cages and are doing just fine on their own. They have been around town for about 10 or 15 years, and Witzeman said the Valley is one of the few areas, perhaps the only one, in the country to have a wild population of the things.

Peach-faced lovebirds are native to Namibia, which I'm pretty sure is in Africa, and neighboring Angola, which I am almost positive is in Africa. Apparently, the climate and the lay of the land in those countries are similar to the Valley's.

The birds nest in eaves and palm trees and the like. Witzeman said the state Game and Fish Department has been keeping an eye on them, because introducing non-native species can be disastrous in some cases. So far, at least, the lovebirds don't seem to be displacing other cavity-nesters, such as woodpeckers.

By Any Name, It's Still Dry
April 22, 2001

Q: *We just moved here from Seattle, and we've already been busted for saying "cho-lla" instead of "choy-a." Now we have a couple of questions. First: What's the difference between a wash and an arroyo? And, arcadia door vs. sliding glass door — what's up with that?*

A: Were you really walking around saying "cho-lla?" Oh, you wacky newcomers. This leads us to believe that we should devote a lesson in the near future to pronunciations.

As to your first question: According to *Essentials of Physical Geography,* (Sixth Edition, by Gabler, Sager, Wise, Petersen; Harcourt College Publishing, 1999) a wash, wadi, arroyo and barranca are all essentially the same thing. To wit: "A generally steep-walled channel of an intermittent stream in an arid region. The stream bed is characteristically choked with coarse alluvium."

We were feeling kind of choked with coarse alluvium just the other day, but after a couple of Tums and a nap, we felt better.

Washes play a valuable role in the desert environment. They are natural flood channels, habitats for many desert plants and highways for many desert animals. Flash floods make them very dangerous places to be during heavy rainstorms, even if the storm is miles away.

As to the second question: Sliding glass doors became popular in the early 1950s. There was at the time in the Valley a company named Arcadia that manufactured such doors, and it is our belief their name became synonymous with sliding glass doors.

The chief functions of such doors are to let in light and burglars. Many arcadia doors can easily be lifted out of their tracks from the outside. You can get inexpensive locks at the hardware store, or you can drill a hole and insert a nail through the inside frame and part way through the metal doorframe.

Strangeness Of Qs Is Quite Scary

May 5, 2001

This being the end of the week, I am clearing up a pile of assorted questions that have been hanging around my desk for a while, perhaps because they got stuck in some barbecue sauce I spilled the other day. As always, the depth and breadth of your interests, the essential oddness of it all, leaves me badly shaken.

Q The First: *Why do Gambel's quail have that funny little topknot on their heads? What's it for?*

I asked several people about this and nobody seemed to know for sure, but the consensus was that the topknot probably is used for behavioral displays — mating, aggression, fear, that sort of thing. We use cell phones.

Q The Second: *I was flying over Lake Pleasant the other day and it looked like large areas of the lake were covered with pond scum. What's going on out there?*

With uncharacteristic restraint, I am not going to involve my masters in this one.

A very nice lady at the Lake Pleasant ranger station named Tiffany Whitehead assured me the lake is not covered with pond scum. However, she said, when boat traffic on the lake is heavy, as it has been with the recent nice weather, it tends to churn up sediment and other crud from below the surface of the lake. This is most common in shallower areas. It all settles back down eventually.

Q The Third: *Is Flagstaff the largest U.S. city at the highest elevation?*

Questions involving the suffix "est" always make me nervous because there is invariably an est-ier answer than the one I come up with.

Having said that, the answer is no. Flagstaff's elevation is 6,894 feet, and its population, according to Census 2000, is 52,894. Santa Fe is at 6,947 feet and has a population of about 68,000. There may be other cities higher and bigger than Santa Fe, but finding them was beginning to border on work and the enterprise was hastily dropped.

Jelly Puts Pyracantha Fears To Rest

May 26, 2001

First of all, I am not taking responsibility for this. If you get sick it's not my fault. I'm just passing on the information.

And I'm not going to start doing recipes all the time, so don't send me any.

Here's the deal: A lady wrote the other day and said that all her life she had been told that pyracantha berries were poisonous, but then she came across a recipe for pyracantha jelly.

I always thought they were poisonous, too, but birds eat them all the time and it doesn't seem to hurt them any. And pyracantha jelly sounds pretty good. I wonder if you can make pyracantha pie.

Several lists of toxic plants I found on the Internet included pyracantha. A few of them said it's not poisonous, but it would make you sick to your stomach.

So I called the Poison Control Center and a very helpful lady there said pyracantha berries are not poisonous, but if you ate a bunch of green ones you'd probably feel sick. She also said pyracantha jelly isn't very good. Too many little seeds.

I am not, as I said, going to start running recipes, but pyracantha jelly sounds so goofy that I am making a one-time exception. So here, courtesy of Syb Mann of Mesa, is a recipe for pyracantha jelly. Remember, don't blame me if it makes you sick. Don't blame Syb Mann, either.

- 1 full pint pyracantha berries
- 2 pints water
- Juice of 1 small grapefruit
- Juice of 1 small lemon
- 1 package powdered pectin
- 5-1/2 cups sugar

If a strong flavor is desired, use 2/3 quart of berries. Boil berries and water, covered, for 20 minutes. Add the grapefruit and lemon juice. Strain to 4-1/2 cups. Add pectin and bring mixture to boil. Add sugar and boil until it jells (about 4 to 5 minutes). Pour into sterile glasses and seal.

Bon appetit.

To Cool Off Outside, Get Hot Inside

May 29, 2001

Today's question: *My husband insists that eating hot, spicy food during hot weather actually helps you cool off. He is wrong about so many other things. Please tell him he is wrong about this. I think he's going to give himself a stroke.*

Sorry, lady. He got this one right. Why do you think a lot of spicy dishes come from hot places, such as Mexico or Thailand or India? Ever think of that? Huh?

When you eat spicy food all sorts of things happen. Your body decides to cool off. Blood vessels close to the surface of your skin, especially on your face and neck, expand so the blood can throw off heat. Your internal temperature goes down while your skin temperature goes up. You sweat, and as the sweat evaporates it cools you off.

And the longer you live in hot weather, the better your body gets at doing all that. That's why when it's cold around here, you hear people saying their blood has thinned out. Your body is just used to cooling off, not warming up.

It's kind of the reverse of why drinking alcohol isn't a good idea in hot weather. Aside from the fact it makes you stupid, alcohol constricts your blood vessels so it's harder for your body to carry heat out from your insides.

So, amazing as it may be, your husband is apparently right about this one. Don't feel bad. As you said, he's probably wrong about plenty of other things.

While we're on the subject, do you know why water never seems to help if you've just set your mouth on fire with a big bite of spicy food?

Because a lot of spicy foods have a lot of oil in them and are often cooked in oil. It coats your lips and tongue and throat, and since oil and water don't mix, that big glass of ice water you just swallowed doesn't wash away the hot stuff. Milk works and so does alcohol, but if neither of those appeal, a piece of bread or a tortilla will smother the flames.

Gen. Irvin McDowell No Fighter
June 10, 2001

Q: *Who was the McDowell in Fort McDowell?*

A: This is an excellent question because it has nothing to do, at least not directly, with Jack Swilling or Darrell Duppa, two worthies of whom we are thoroughly sick and tired.

Fort McDowell was founded in 1865 at the juncture of Sycamore Creek and the Verde River by five companies of the army's California Volunteers. It was near several Indian trails and convenient for expeditions against the Yavapai and Tonto Apache, who were tearing up the pea patch at the time.

It was named for Gen. Irvin McDowell, the commanding officer of the Department of California and New Mexico. He held this post because it was about as far away from the Civil War as his superiors could put him.

Born in Ohio in 1818, McDowell was a West Point graduate and a veteran of the Mexican War. He was a skilled administrator but a remarkable failure in the field. It was McDowell who commanded the Union army at the first battle of Bull Run, where he proved to be one very sorry pooch indeed. Demoted to a division command, he returned for the second battle of Bull Run. In the debacle that followed, he was especially singled out for remarkable ineptitude. Although an official inquiry later cleared him, it was the end of his career as a field commander, and he was shipped West. He died in San Francisco in 1882.

Fort McDowell was abandoned in 1881 and became the Fort McDowell Indian Reservation in 1890.

As a military post, it was not a choice assignment. Historian Marshall Trimble quotes this lament from one officer posted there:

"Four years I have sat here and looked at the Four Peaks, and I'm getting almighty tired of it."

Is 8 Degrees Worth Drive To Tucson?

June 13, 2001

Today's question: *If Tucson and Phoenix are both in the desert, why is it always just a little bit cooler in Tucson than it is in the Valley?*

We'll get to that in a minute, but first a few words about the hot-weather limerick contest: It's that fifth line that's killing some of you. It has to rhyme with the first two.

And the fifth line should have something to do with the other four. One guy was going great until the fifth line where he announced that everyone was eaten by wolves. Eaten by wolves?

Anyway, Tucson is usually a little bit cooler than Phoenix because it is a little bit higher up. You may not actually have a sense of ascending when you drive there because you are lulled into a state of semi-consciousness because it is the most boring drive in the world.

Phoenix's elevation is 1,107 feet. Tucson's is 2,550. Air cools as it rises because the pressure on it drops. Rising air cools at a rate of 5.4 degrees per 1,000 feet and sinking air warms at the same rate. That is called the dry adiabatic lapse rate.

Adiabatic is a good word, don't you think? It means that heat is not being added or taken away, but since not many people probably know that, you could use it anyway you want. As in: "My car needs more adiabatic." Or "Your tie is too adiabatic."

So the dry adiabatic lapse rate would mean that all else being equal, you could expect Tucson to be about 8 degrees cooler than the Valley.

That's nice for the people who live there, I suppose, but I'm still not sure it's worth the drive.

So let's review what we've learned so far:
The dry adiabatic lapse rate
Is a standard that I think is just great.
It means air gets more chilly
When it goes uphilly
And then they all were eaten by wolves.

The Edible, Inevitable 'sa-War-O'
July 15, 2001

Here at the Valley 101 Research Center and Windshield Squeegeeing Service, we have amassed a collection of three questions about saguaros, those noble cactuses that symbolize Arizona just as surely as do recall elections.

And we now endeavor to answer these queries with, as always, the help of Patrick Quirk of the Desert Botanical Gardens, who has forgotten more about saguaros then you'll ever know.

I have lived here almost all my life, but this year was the first time I've seen saguaros with red flowers. Usually these are paler blooms. Is there a reason for the red?

Those were not flowers. What you saw was the saguaro fruit that had split open to show its pulpy interior.

Saguaro fruit was an important part of the diets of many Native American peoples hereabouts. They even made a kind of wine from it. For some tribes, the saguaro harvest, followed by the life-giving monsoon rains, marked the beginning of the new year.

Why do saguaros have different numbers of arms?

Why not? Why do trees have different numbers of branches?

However, a healthy and well-watered saguaro will have more arms than a thirsty or ailing saguaro.

When you drive west into California on Interstate 10 the saguaro cactus seem to stop precisely at the border. What's the cause of this?

As you travel east to west across Arizona, it gets drier, and the saguaros get scarcer. Phoenix's average annual rainfall is 7.66 inches. Yuma's is 3.17.

The monsoon rains that saguaros need to germinate and grow just don't reach that far west.

And by the time you get to the California line, the saguaros you see tend to be somewhat spindly things confined to washes or other rare wet spots.

One last thing: a tip for the newly arrived. It's "suh-WAR-o." Nothing will cause hot coals of scorn and ridicule to be heaped on your head more quickly than pronouncing it "sa-gar-o."

Valley Had Its Share Of Ranches
July 22, 2001

Q: *There are so many places around the Valley with "ranch" in the name. How many were ever really ranches?*

A: Lots of them. Lots and lots. Despite all the sprawl, you have to bear in mind that the Valley metro area started as a farming community, and until fairly recently, Maricopa County was primarily an agricultural area. So there were a lot of ranches.

Not all of these spreads were exactly hardscrabble kinds of places.

McCormick Ranch in Scottsdale, before it turned into a residential development, was the home of Fowler and Anne McCormick. Fowler McCormick's two grandfathers were Cyrus McCormick, the inventor of the grain reaper, and John D. Rockefeller, so he wasn't exactly hurting for cash. He later became president and chairman of the board of International Harvester.

In his day, the 4,200-acre site was a working ranch, and the McCormicks raised Black Angus cattle. After Anne McCormick's death, the ranch was sold in 1970 to Kaiser-Aetna. That company later sold off 1,120 acres, which is now known as Scottsdale Ranch.

Gainey Ranch, another ritzy Scottsdale address, was once a 640-acre Arabian horse ranch owned by Daniel C. Gainey. In fact, over the years three Daniel Gaineys owned the place. Most of it was sold in 1980 to Markland Properties for residential development, but the family held on to 80 acres to have a place to stable their horses during the annual All-Arabian Horse Show. The Gainey Trust later developed that site for retail and residential use.

In their day, the Gaineys entertained lavishly in their Moorish-style home, movie stars, political bigshots and jet-setters drawn to Scottsdale for the horse show. The home later became the private Daniel C. Gainey Estate Club.

Misters Play Minor Role In Humidity

July 31, 2001

Today's question: *My mother wants to know whether the widespread use of misting systems has any effect on humidity levels?*

I also have at hand a letter from a guy whose mother told him that if you eat something that's been kept cold in a refrigerator in a metal container you will die. I like your mother better.

In short, the answer is no. Even I could figure that out. This, however, makes for sort of a short column so I passed your mom's question on to David Runyan of the National Weather Service's Phoenix office. He is extremely smart.

"Misters are very small scale," he said. "Thus the effects likewise are small."

Actually, he didn't say that. He wrote it in an e-mail, a very thoughtful note on intentional or unintentional things people do that affect the weather.

"In the immediate vicinity of the mister, the relative humidity obviously increases. Multiply that by 100 or 1,000, the cumulative effect grows.

"But at any one given moment, there is something like 20,160 cubic miles (48 miles by 35 miles by 12 miles) of air over the Phoenix metropolitan area. That air mass is always in a state of flux, mixing upward, downward and into and out of the region," Runyan wrote.

Didn't I tell you he was smart? Just figuring out that cubic-miles thing was a pretty good trick.

So the gist of it is that there is so much air out there and so much air coming and going all the time that misting systems don't make that much difference.

If anything, he said, it's more likely that irrigation would impact the weather more than misting systems might although apparently nobody has studied that around here. In the 1970s, there was a study of weather patterns over areas of Texas, Kansas and Nebraska that determined "unusual pockets of hail and tornadoes were found that may be associated with heavily irrigated regions."

So tell your mother to mist away. And ask her if she ever heard about that metal dish in the refrigerator thing.

Desert Toad Can Threaten Dog's Health

August 2, 2001

Today's question: *We recently had to rush our Doberman pinscher to an emergency veterinary clinic because he went into convulsions after trying to bite a Sonoran desert toad. I think you should warn people about this.*

Really? Well, I think I should warn people that you can't patch a crack in your car radiator with duct tape, especially if it's really hot.

This came as a major disappointment, plus I burned my fingers and I looked like an idiot when the Highway Patrol guy stopped to see why I was hopping up and down on the side of the road with my fingers in my mouth.

However, if you are more worried about Sonoran desert toads, here goes.

Sonoran desert toads, or *Bufo alvarius*, are ugly brutes that also are known as Colorado River toads. Some people have tried to get high by licking them. Mostly they just got sick.

This is a good time of year for Sonoran desert toads. They spend most of the year underground in holes that they dig themselves or in an abandoned rodent burrow. When it gets rainy, they emerge, croak a lot, breed, eat enough to tide them over for a long time and then go back underground.

They can grow up to 7 inches across and live in Arizona, southeast California and parts of Mexico. They eat insects, spiders and other toads. They're just as ugly as sin, but I guess it isn't often that you see a good-looking toad of any type.

You might come across one on a hike or they may be attracted to your swimming pool, and this is where your dog comes in.

The skin of *Bufo alvarius* produces a toxin that reacts with mucus. If a dog mouths one of these beasts, it can cause paralysis or death. You'll know what's happened because the dog will be pawing at its mouth and salivating a lot.

This can happen even if the toad sits in the dog's water dish for a long time and the dog drinks from it. If I found one of these things in a dog's water dish, I'd sell the house and move. They're gross.

Explaining Clams, Fish In Canals
August 5, 2001

Today we have two questions about the Valley's canal system. This is not surprising. The canals always seem to be of interest to newcomers. That's probably because any body of moving water attracts attention in this sere environment.

Sere is a very good word. According to the Valley 101 Department of Entomology, it means "dried up or withered."

We were surprised they knew that because entomology is the study of bugs. Etymology is the study of words. We always get those two mixed up.

Anyway, the questions: *Where do they get those little seashells that cover the banks of the canals? Is there some place I can buy them?*

And:

Is fishing allowed in the canals, and, if so, is it safe to eat fish from the canals?

One thing at a time. The shells are those of the Asiatic clams, *corbicula fluminea,* that live in the canals, said Scott Harelson, a spokesman for the Salt River Project, which operates 131 miles of canals in the Valley. From time to time, SRP dredges the canals and spreads the sediment on the banks. The clamshells come up with the sediment.

As to the fish, SRP is not exactly thrilled with the idea of you fishing in the canals because of safety issues.

And it is illegal to be in or on the water of the canals. However, it is not illegal to fish in the canals.

One thing: The canals are well-stocked, at considerable expense, with white amurs, an Asian fish that eats weeds and thus keeps the canals flowing. It is not legal to keep a white amur you take from the canals. Frankly, we cannot imagine why you would want to do so anyway, unless perhaps you are thinking of starting a rival canal system.

As to the other fish, there are, among other things, carp, bass, catfish and sometimes trout in the canals, and you may keep what you catch.

"There is no problem eating them. It's just lake water. It would be like fishing at Saguaro Lake," Harelson said.

Palms Count On Roots To Stay Steady

August 8, 2001

Today's question: *Why don't palm trees blow down in strong wind as often as other trees do?*

I thought this was going to be an easy one, and I was prepared to pad it out with a lot of cheap jokes about my masters. Instead, it got kind of complicated, so I had to cut out the jokes, which is just as well because I would have had to explain them to my masters anyway.

This is the deal: Palm trees are monocots as opposed to other trees, such as paloverdes or oaks, which are dicots.

Kim Stone, a horticulturist at the Boyce Thompson Arboretum near Superior, went to some pains to explain the differences to me. He is a very patient man.

Basically, monocots, which include grasses, orchids, irises and other stuff, have embryos that sprout straight up in a single shoot, instead of up and out with branches, as dicots do.

A palm grows straight up, gaining its height on overlapping leaf bases. Hence, it doesn't have branches to catch the wind. A big, branchy Norfolk Island pine, on the other hand, would just as soon blow over as look at you.

If you took a cross section of a palm tree, you would find a number of brownish spots instead of the growth rings like you'd find in a dicot. These are bundles of vascular strands that carry nutrients up and down the tree. It's like a thick steel cable woven from a lot of smaller steel wires.

This is starting to make my brain hurt.

Anyway, each strand in these vascular bundles is connected to the root system. Dicots have woody roots, and in most dicots, 80 percent of the root system is within the top two feet of soil.

Anyone who has ever tried to dig up a palm can tell you it has fibrous roots that not only fan out to great distances but also go down deep. Like to somewhere down around the tectonic plates.

So all this combines to give a palm tree a very solid base in the ground and a very supple trunk that will bend in the wind without breaking.

Evaporation Rate is Just Dead Weight

August 9, 2001

Today's question: *How much water do I lose from my swimming pool through evaporation?*

This is a question that comes in a lot, evaporation from swimming pools or from Tempe Town Lake. It seems to be preying on the minds of many of you.

Personally, in terms of swimming pools, I thought last year's question about how to make chicken soup in your pool was more interesting, but there you have it. If you want evaporation, you'll get evaporation.

I actually found an equation for this used by the American Society of Heating, Refrigeration and Air-Conditioning Engineers. To wit: "W = (95+0.425 v) (pw-pa)Y, where W is evaporation rate, lb/h ft2; v is air velocity at water surface, ft/min.; pw is saturation vapor pressure at water temperature, in. Hg; pa is saturation vapor pressure at air dew point, in. Hg; and Y is latent heat at pool temperature, Btu/lb."

If you think I am going to explain this, much less attempt to work it out, for what I get paid, you are sorely mistaken.

According to the city of Tempe's Web site, water evaporates from open bodies of water in the Valley at a rate of 6.2 acre-feet per acre of surface per year. That's about 2 million gallons. The annual loss from Town Lake would be around 1,388 acre-feet. An acre-foot is an acre of water 1 foot deep.

I suppose I could extrapolate from that the evaporation rate for a residential pool, but given my math skills, that would be sort of a dubious enterprise. Instead, I called a bunch of people who sell pool covers, and they said that in the summer a typical residential pool would lose from three-quarters of an inch to an inch of water a day.

I think, but I'm not sure, that you could check this out by floating a bucket of water in your pool for a day and then measuring how much was lost from the bucket. At least that sounds plausible.

If you are worried about the bucket tipping over, you could anchor it with some dead weight. One of my masters, for instance.

It's True: You Can Sunburn Underwater

August 17, 2001

Today's question: *We are recent transplants to Arizona from Washington, where it rains a lot, so we never had to worry about this before: Can you get sunburned under the water?*

I will answer that in a moment, but first I need to remind you that as new Arizonans and pool owners, it is your duty to sit by the pool on Thanksgiving Day and call relatives in colder climates and say, "Hey, guess what we're doing?"

Anyway, the answer is yes. Even if various parts of your body parts are submerged, they are still susceptible to sunburn.

As you no doubt know, it is the ultraviolet rays in sunshine that cause sunburn. Clouds or fog or water block out some of those rays, but still up to 70 or 80 percent beam through.

One source I found said ultraviolet rays can penetrate clear water to a depth of 25 centimeters, and of course 25 centimeters is the same as 9.85 miles. Wait, that can't be right. Inches, it's the same as 9.85 inches.

There is also the question of reflection. If you're bobbing in the pool with sunscreen smeared all over your bald spot, you can still end up sunburned because some of the ultraviolet rays are bouncing off the water and smacking you in the face.

There are a number of precautions you might take. First, you could keep rotting vegetation in your pool to cloud the water.

This would be yucky, but it would keep harmful rays from penetrating as deeply as they would in clear water.

Or you could swim fully clothed, including a hat and gloves. This might be better than the rotting vegetation idea.

Or, and this might be best, you could coat yourself with the best, water-resistant sunscreen you can find. Get one with an SPF of 15 or higher and make sure the label says it protects from both UVA and UVB, which are the two bands of ultraviolet light that burn us.

And don't forget about that Thanksgiving thing. Mark it on your calendar now.

Yes, God Has Sense Of Humor

August 23, 2001

I was not going to do any more on lightning, having pretty well beat the topic to death Wednesday, but I just had a call from a reader with a question that was so pleasingly odd that I decided to check it out. To wit:

Is it true that lightning is good for citrus?

Isn't that a great question? It's goofy with just that faint whiff of plausibility that gets you wondering if there is really something to it.

Well, there isn't. It's hooey.

James Truman, manager of the University of Arizona's experimental citrus farm, said he has never heard of such a thing. He did, however, speculate that years with plenty of rain, which might also mean lots of lightning, would in general be good for citrus because the rainwater would contain a certain amount of nitrogen.

And as long as we're on the subject of citrus, do you know what an orange dog is? Neither did I until I did a recent column on why bird poop is white.

An orange dog is the caterpillar of the giant swallowtail butterfly and feeds exclusively on citrus. The thing about it is that it looks exactly like bird poop. Is that great or what? Further proof that God has a sense of humor.

If you were to find an orange dog on your citrus tree and poke it, it would shoot out a little tongue that gives off some sort of defensive chemical. Of course, unless you're good at it, you might have to poke a lot of real bird poop before you found an orange dog.

Orange dogs are good eaters and are especially fond of young leaves. However, they also are preyed upon by a number of teeny-tiny parasitic insects, so it's not likely that they would get around to doing much serious damage to your trees.

The ones that survive turn into giant swallowtails, which are, of course, giant and also very beautiful. They're about four inches across, yellow and brown, and don't look a bit like bird poop.

Warning: Read This With Caution
August 29, 2001

I do not apologize for what follows, nor do I condone it. It may please you or it may make you angry. It could drive you to do injury to yourself or those around you. I take no responsibility either way.

I received this item in the mail last week. The correspondent provided a name, address and phone number. I decline to print any of those, lest angry mobs of villagers appear at her house and menace her with pitchforks, clubs or torches. Worse yet, others might try to contact her and encourage her in endeavors such as this.

The address, I will say, was that of a home in a quiet residential area somewhere in the Valley. The handwriting was clear and firm, the grammar and spelling good.

There were no signs, at least outwardly, that the correspondent had been institutionalized at any time and no outward signs of substance abuse, childhood trauma or recent head injury. However, if you happen to know the author of this story or happen to meet her, I would advise approaching her with caution.

One last thing: I am by no means printing this to encourage others to send in similar stories. I print this as a cautionary message, perhaps a signpost on our slow journey downhill to utter degradation.

The author said she was writing in response to a recent column on fishing in the canals. She said she felt compelled to comment on "the inherent dangers" of the canals.

What follows is an exact transcript of an excerpt from her letter. Before you read it, please make sure you have read and clearly understand all the disclaimers above. She wrote:

"Recently I was leaning over a canal bridge abutment, and my wallet fell out of my coat's breast pocket and plummeted toward the water.

"As it hit, a large carp surfaced, grabbed the wallet and flipped its head. The billfold flew to another larger carp and then on to a third!

"I was astonished! This was the first time I'd ever seen carp-to-carp walleting."

McDowells Aren't Blast From Past

August 31, 2001

Today's question: *I have a nice view of the McDowell Mountains. Sometimes they look like a mountain range, and sometimes, in certain light, they look like a group of individual volcanic cones. Which are they?*

I have in my pile a fair number of volcano questions that have come in over the months. I never seem to get around to answering them, usually because they involve terms such as "Cenozoic Laramide gneiss," and I get tired just thinking about stuff like that.

However, there was pie for breakfast today, so with firm purpose and cheerful mien we shall now take up this matter of the McDowells.

According to one of my favorite books, *Roadside Geology of Arizona* by Halka Chronic, the McDowells are "rocky hills (that) protrude through the gravel," so I guess that means they are not mountains or volcanoes, just rocky hills. I suppose we should call them mountains anyway because the McDowell Rocky Hills wouldn't be much of a name. On the other hand, Halka Chronic is a great name, don't you think?

According to Chronic, the McDowells are mostly composed of Miocene stream deposits. Miocene is the fourth epoch of the Tertiary Period in the Cenozoic Era. Really. I looked it up. The Miocene was between 5 million and 24 million years ago.

Arizona has many volcanoes, but none of them obviously are doing much right now.

The Superstitions were once part of a whole complex of volcanoes. The San Francisco Peaks near Flagstaff are volcanic and so are many other mountain ranges around the state. In fact, the Grand Canyon was created by a volcano. Not really. I just wondered if you were paying attention.

Sunset Crater, just north of Flagstaff, might be one of Arizona's newer volcanoes. It is a cinder cone, a great big pile of ash and cinders that piles up around a volcanic vent. It blew about 1,000 years ago, the blink of an eye, Cenozoically speaking.

That Water You Spied Is Grusp
September 2, 2001

Q: *If the Salt River is dry, what is that water in the riverbed you see when you fly into Sky Harbor from the east or take off from the west?*

A: We were not immediately certain of the answer because here at the Valley 101 Research Center it is our firm policy to close our eyes during takeoffs and landings at Sky Harbor or any other airport. Sometimes we sob quietly, too.

But we digress.

The ponds you see are part of the Granite Reef Underground Storage Project, a partnership among the Salt River Project, the Salt River Pima-Maricopa Indian Community and the cities of Phoenix, Mesa, Scottsdale, Tempe, Chandler and Gilbert. The facility is operated by SRP on Indian land just west of the Granite Reef Dam.

The idea is simple: They pour water into the ground so they can pump it out and use it later, if need be.

The water stored there is part of Arizona's allocation of Colorado River water delivered to the Valley by the Central Arizona Project.

When CAP water first started flowing here in the early 1990s, there basically was no place to put it all. For years, some interests had hoped to build a huge dam, Orme Dam, at the junction of the Salt and Verde rivers and put the water there.

We do not wish to be too technical here, but this turned out to be, for many reasons, a dumb idea. At the same time, there was growing interest in underground storage.

Since GRUSP, pronounced "grusp," was completed in 1994, about 500,000 acre-feet of water have seeped into the East Valley's natural aquifer. Last year alone, GRUSP received about 90,000 acre-feet. (An acre-foot is 325,850 gallons, about as much as a typical family uses in a year.)

This is not the only underground storage facility around. The Central Arizona Project has developed several others since 1992. However, GRUSP is one of the largest such projects in the country.

Roadrunner Food Habits Are A Bash

September 5, 2001

Today's question: *I've seen roadrunners running around with lizards in their mouths, but recently, I was surprised to see one grab a small bird, bash it against the ground several times and take off into the desert with the body. Is this normal?*

Grabbed it and bashed it on the ground several times? I hope this doesn't give my masters any ideas.

Yes, what you saw was perfectly normal, at least for roadrunners.

They cannot live by lizards alone. They also eat scorpions, snakes, rodents, small birds, eggs, insects and a few berries and seeds every now and then just to keep regular.

Roadrunners are not delicate creatures. They usually kill their prey by picking it up by the head with their beak and walloping it on a rock or the hard ground until it is dead. Then the bird swallows it whole.

In the case of something tough like a horned toad, a roadrunner might spend 10 or 15 minutes whacking it on the ground to kill it.

They have such quick reflexes that they have been known to snatch hummingbirds and dragonflies out of the air in midflight. Hummingbirds and dragonflies probably don't find this to be all that great, but you have to admit it would be something to see.

They catch rattlesnakes by spreading their wings out like a matador's cape to keep the snake guessing. Then they grab it by the tail and flail it around until it's dead. This is kind of gross: If the snake is too big to swallow whole, the roadrunner walks around with the corpse dangling out of its mouth as it digests the other end.

I'm always surprised at how many people have lived here a long time without ever seeing a roadrunner. They prefer the wide open spaces where their speed — up to 15 mph — works to their advantage.

A Whopper On A Whale In Arizona

September 9, 2001

Today, students, we take up one of our favorite kinds of topics here at the Valley 101 Research Laboratory and Used Computer Parts Clearance Center: an outlandish story that cannot be proved but still might be true.

We love these kinds of stories because they involve a minimum amount of actual work, while still offering some entertainment, thus freeing us for study of other topics, such as a seven-letter word for "Asian yellow gum resin" (gamboge). Today's topic is the great Mesa whale skeleton. This is a persistent piece of Valley folklore that holds that sometime in the 1850s the carcass of a whale was found on the banks of the Salt River somewhere in the vicinity of present-day Mesa.

Supposedly, the leviathan somehow came up the Colorado River from the Gulf of California during a great flood, hung a right at the Gila and eventually came to rest on the banks of the Salt.

This is a nearly perfect piece of hooey. Perfect in that while it is outrageous, there is no way of saying for certain that it didn't happen. After all, this is Arizona, a land of odd and marvelous things.

And, as the eminently eminent historian Marshall Trimble pointed out, there wasn't much of anyone around here then to say yea or nay to the whale whopper. "It seems nigh impossible, but who knows?" Trimble said.

Bob McCord, curator of natural history at the Mesa Southwest Museum, said he has tried many times to track down this tale. "I can find no primary source that can confirm it," said he. The museum does have some whale bones, but these were contraband seized by authorities many years ago and turned over to the museum.

McCord noted that 3 million years ago the Gulf of California extended as far north as Parker, and fossil remains of a fish akin to the grunion have been found thereabouts. But a whale in the Salt? No.

Or at least, probably not.

So What If Your Pool's A Little Cold?

September 21, 2001

Today's question: *It's still hot out, around 100 every day. Why is my swimming pool very cold all of the sudden?*

There are a number of possible explanations, some of which may be correct.

No offense, but it's possible you are a cold-temperature wuss, one of those people who can't handle anything cooler than bath water, and that a slight change in the water temperature leaves you freezing. That's one possibility.

Another possibility is that with the end of the monsoon, the air is drier, and thus there is more evaporation. Evaporation cools the surface of the water. In August, the average dew point, the temperature at which water condenses out of the air, was 61.1 degrees. Through Tuesday, the average dew point for September is 45. This is the reason your evaporative cooler is working again.

And the drier air makes it easier for the heat of the day to radiate away from the ground at night. This means the nights are getting cooler. The average low for August was 83.9. Through Tuesday, the average low for September has been 81.3. Water holds heat well, but over the long run, even a few degrees will make a difference in the temperature of your pool.

And, day by day, your pool is getting less warmth from the sun. Saturday at 4:05 p.m. is the autumnal equinox. At that time, the sun will be directly over the equator, headed south.

The equinox means that day and night will be of equal length, but because of our latitude, that won't happen here until Wednesday, when the sun will rise at 6:19 a.m. and set at 6:19 p.m. From then until Dec. 21, the days will get shorter, and the nights will get longer, and your pool will get colder.

You could get a wet suit, I suppose, but you'd probably look kind of silly in it. Pool heaters can be a bit expensive, but you can probably afford one of those pool covers that hold in the heat. Or you could just bite the bullet and jump in, you wuss.

Yes, Camels Roamed Wild In Arizona

October 7, 2001

Q: *We just moved here from the Midwest. My son came home from his new school the other day and said there are wild camels living in the desert. Is this true?*

A: Your son is no doubt a charming lad, but he needs to pay closer attention in class if he hopes to live up to Arizona's exacting education standards, standards that have won us the sobriquet of the "Mississippi of the West."

At one time, many years ago, there were indeed camels roaming the deserts of Arizona.

Before the railroads came to the state, Jefferson Davis, then the Secretary of War, took it in his head that the answer to transportation problems in the region was camels. Subsequently, buyers were dispatched to the Mideast, and in 1856, the first of the beasts arrived in the Southwest.

Davis was correct. The camels were ideally suited for the Arizona desert, especially after Arab camel drivers were imported to handle them.

The best known of these was one Hadji Ali, who became known as Hi Jolly. Unlike many of his colleagues, Hadji Ali remained in the United States until his death in 1902. In a cemetery in Quartzsite there is a pyramid-shaped monument, topped by a camel, in his honor.

The camels, as noted above, were a success. Army surveying teams, freight haulers and others in need of beasts of burden found that camels could carry more weight farther than any mule and could live off what little vegetation grew on those arid grounds.

However, with the advent of the Civil War, the camel project was discontinued. Some of the beasts were sold to mining interests, but many were simply turned loose in the desert. It is not known for how many years these feral camels survived, but it was long enough to earn a page in Arizona history.

Lizards Can High-Tail It On 2 Legs
October 10, 2001

Today's question: *I was at Lake Pleasant recently, and I thought I saw a lizard running across some rocks as fast as can be upright on its back legs. Was I hallucinating?*

I don't know. Do you hallucinate often? I was waiting at a stoplight once and thought I saw Mr. Peanut — you know, the Planters peanuts guy — in the next car.

I thought I was hallucinating, but when I looked again, it really was a guy in a Mr. Peanut costume. I wonder where he got it. That would be a pretty cool thing to have.

Anyway, no, you were not hallucinating, at least not in this case. Nor should the idea of coldblooded vertebrates with small brains and reptilian nervous systems moving on two legs seem too remarkable. Look at my masters, for instance.

It is likely that what you saw was a zebratail lizard or a leopard lizard, which are related to iguanas and are fairly common around here.

Zebratails grow to 6 to 9 inches long and have black bars on the undersides of their tails. The book I looked them up in said that they are extremely hard to catch, but then I don't know why you'd want to catch one anyway.

Leopard lizards are bigger, up to 15 inches, and are gray and brown with dark spots all over. Both kinds eat insects and other lizards and whatever else is handy.

The reason these lizards and some others sometimes run on their back legs is simple: It's faster.

This I learned from the always-helpful Bill Sloan of the Arizona Herpetological Association. They usually run on only two legs when they are in a special hurry, such as when they are being pursued by predators.

Actually, lizards were on their own two feet long before humans. The fossil record shows lizards that were bipedal 80 million years ago.

And in South America, the basilisk lizard, also known as the Jesus Christ lizard, can run on water at up to 6 mph, which has to be a pretty good trick. But if I had to choose, I'd rather have a Mr. Peanut costume.

Cold Spots Give Reason For Pause
October 19, 2001

Today's question: *My neighbor and I walk our dogs along the same route every evening, and there are always a few spots where the temperature is suddenly 3 to 5 degrees cooler. These areas are very small, but you definitely can feel the air there is cooler. This isn't the difference between a warm sidewalk and cool grass. Some of these spots are in the middle of lawns or empty lots. What causes this?*

Boy, that's a long question. As luck would have it, I knew the answer right off the bat. This woman and her friend obviously are walking across portals to the underworld, hidden gates to the nether regions. I'm surprised she didn't mention anything about the dogs whimpering or cringing when they pass these spots.

This answer makes sense to me. I think it is related somehow to the fact that the room temperature always drops a few degrees when one of my masters walks by.

Unfortunately, this answer turned out to be wrong, which I learned by consulting with the King of the Weather Wonks, Randy Cerveny of Arizona State University.

These two dog walkers, it develops, are experiencing adventures in microclimatology, highly localized weather conditions.

For example, in the summer the Arcadia neighborhood of east-central Phoenix always seems to be about 5 degrees cooler than other parts of town, probably because of the many trees and lush lawns there.

The cold spots probably are small depressions or low spots in the terrain. They could be so slight they are not even noticed. The temperature in these areas is lower because cold air, being denser than warm air, settles there in the same way that water seeks its own level.

Cold air, as we all know, is denser than warm air because its little molecules aren't bouncing around and expanding as much as they would if they were heated. This is why you never hear about anyone going for a cold-air balloon ride.

Elucidating About Coots And Grackles

November 8, 2001

Today's question: *I was born and raised in Phoenix. I grew up with cactus wrens, roadrunners and quail, but where did all these grackles come from? A friend of mine says they were always here, but I think they are a recent occurrence. Can you elucidate?*

I can now say that I looked up "elucidate."

This is one of several grackle questions I have received lately, and I take it up with some trepidation. A year or so ago I wrote some less than complimentary things about grackles and received a number of calls and letters from people who actually like grackles. I can't imagine why, but there you have it.

This is the time of year for grackle questions because this is the time of year when grackles congregate, especially in the evening, in big flocks to poop on things and exchange the news of the day at the top of their lungs.

Anyway, in answer to your question, great-tailed grackles have been moving north from Mexico for years. The first record of them in Maricopa County was three birds spotted near Peoria in 1954. By 1970 they were considered common.

Common grackles, which are even less desirable than great-tailed grackles, are another story. They have been moving west since European colonists began turning forest land into farmland. They are still mostly found east of the Rockies, but there have been sightings in Maricopa County.

Another bird question:

How do coots migrate? They are arriving in a pond near my house, but they seem to only be able to fly well enough to hop from the water to the shore.

How do coots migrate? I bet you thought I was going to say something like, "By RV." Aren't you just a little bit ashamed of yourself?

Coots, the water birds, are found year-round in the Valley, but their numbers increase in the cooler months.

They are not graceful birds. They look more like chickens than ducks. However, they can fly. Maybe the ones you saw were just tired.

'The' Black Canyon Is North of City

November 18, 2001

Today's question: *Where exactly is Black Canyon, anyway?*

Which one? I found four Black Canyons in *Arizona Names, X Marks the Spot*, which is a really swell book, by the way. In fact, there are about six pages of "Black" names in there: Black Springs, Black Knob, Black Creek, Black Draw, Black Mesa, Black Gulch, Black-Hearted Dimwitted Masters, etc., etc. OK, I made up the last one.

I wonder why there are so many "Black" names. It could be the nature of the rock or maybe it's the dramatic shadows caused by the light in these parts. Someone should look into this.

Anyway, I assume you are talking about Black Canyon, as in the Black Canyon Freeway, a.k.a. Interstate 17.

You know that Sunset Point rest stop on the west side of I-17 between New River and Cordes Junction? It's a great rest stop, although if you're leaving town, it's really too soon to stop and if your headed back to town, you're almost there anyway. Of course, this depends on how old your kids are or how much coffee you've had.

Anyway, when you look west at the Sunset Point rest stop, you're looking down into Black Canyon. The mountains across the way are the Bradshaws.

According to the *Roadside Geology of Arizona*, another swell book, the canyon has dark metamorphic rocks that are about 1.7 million years old. Metamorphic means rocks made from older rocks that have been subjected to great heat or pressure.

The old Black Canyon Highway used to be the main road out of town headed north. It went through New River, Black Canyon City, Mayer and Dewey and so forth. There was stagecoach service of one kind or another between Prescott and Phoenix on the old Black Canyon road until 1917.

There are still plenty of old guys around who will chew your ear off with stories about driving the old Black Canyon Highway, so be careful who you ask about it.

Don't Scoff At Our Birds, Newcomer

December 12, 2001

Today's question: *We moved here four months ago, and we love it. But this is what bothers me: Why are the birds here so drab? Why aren't there any brightly colored birds?*

I don't know if I should answer this or not. Drab? Guy just moves here and probably doesn't even have Arizona plates yet, and he's putting the bad mouth on our birds.

This question came in on my voice mail, and the caller did not leave a number so I don't know where he used to live. Maybe he lived in Borneo or some rain forest where they have parrots and whatchamacallits, those Froot Loops birds.

I put this question to the very helpful Janet Witzeman, who is a co-author of the very helpful *Birds of Phoenix and Maricopa County.* She pointed out that most birds common to urban areas are rather plain. Pigeons, thrashers, house sparrows, grackles — these are not exactly dazzling.

However, if you look in your own back yard or, depending on how high the fence is, your neighbors' back yard, you will find plenty of colors. House finches have a nice red breast. There are feral flocks of peach-faced lovebirds in many Valley neighborhoods. Verdins are a common urban bird and have yellow heads and red shoulders.

And, of course, there are hummingbirds. How much more color could you want?

Witzeman also pointed out that, if this gentleman were to walk in the desert, he would find plenty of colorful birds. We have, to name a few, cardinals, lesser goldfinches, scrub jays at higher elevations and kestrels, which get my vote for best all-around bird.

Speaking of jays, I didn't know this until the other day: Birds have black, red, yellow and other pigments but no blue pigment. The blue is caused by light being scattered by microscopic structures in the feathers, like a prism. That's cool.

Why, Yes, Arizona Has A Santa Claus

December 23, 2001

It is taking all my willpower and what little dignity I have left not to do the whole yes-Virginia thing on this one, but as a matter of fact, yes, there is a Santa Claus, Ariz. That is to say, a place in Arizona called Santa Claus.

Granted, it isn't much of a place. In fact, it's closed. But in its heyday, if you could call it that, Santa Claus was quite the attraction.

What's left of the site is on U.S. 93 about 14 miles north of Kingman. It once had a post office, the Christmas Tree Inn, a couple of other Christmas-y sort of buildings, and Santa Clauses on duty year-round.

Santa Claus was the brainstorm of Nina Talbot, a Los Angeles woman who weighed 300 pounds. Really. She advertised that she was the biggest real estate agent in California. I read that in *Arizona Names: X Marks the Spot.*

Anyway, she and her husband moved to Kingman in the 1930s and operated a motel there before she got the idea for Santa Claus in 1937.

The plan was to subdivide the 80-acre site and turn it into a resort town. Obviously, this never happened. Talbot sold the site in 1949 and it kicked around among other developers and dreamers for many years afterward. One guy had a plan for houses on one-acre lots and roads with names like Santa Street and Prancer Parkway and Donner Drive.

The post office, long since closed, used to be a very popular place this time of year because kids would send their letters to Santa there, and thousands of people wanted their cards postmarked from Santa Claus.

The site's popularity started going downhill in the '70s and '80s, and it has been closed for several years.

As long as we are on the subject, there is also, of course, a Christmas, Ariz., which my colleague David Casstevens wrote about a few weeks ago. It's in Gila County.

And there is Christmas Park near Flagstaff, and there is Christmas Tree Lake in Apache County, and there is Merry Christmas to you.

Tumbling Tumbleweeds Ride On Wind

January 15, 2002

Today's question: *Are tumbleweeds a specific plant or is that a generic term for any dead plant that is blown around by the wind?*

New to these parts, stranger? Actually, so are tumbleweeds, relatively speaking.

Tumbleweeds really are a specific plant, the mature form of the Russian thistle, *Salsola iberica*. We think of them as being a real symbol of the West: wide-open spaces and the Sons of the Pioneers and all that. The fact of the matter is tumbleweeds are immigrants from the steppes of Asia. I didn't know that before, even though during my Wonder Bread years I spent many extremely boring hours digging them out of the ancestral estate.

The first seeds arrived in the Dakotas sometime in the 1870s in shipments of wheat or flaxseed from Russia. They were on the West Coast by 1900. They are considered to be peregrinating plants — highly traveled. Russian thistles now are found in about 19 countries outside Asia.

They do not compete well with native plants in undisturbed areas, but give them a farm field or ditch and they'll move right in. They also do well in salty soil. The name Salsola comes from the Latin word for salt. They can grow to be as big as small cars.

In the late 1930s, tumbleweeds completely engulfed the small town of Lester in western Maricopa County. Several chickens were smothered, and the townsite had to be abandoned.

I made that up.

The whole tumbling business is, of course, how the plant disperses its seeds. When the thistle is mature, it dries up, snaps off from its roots with the help of special cells in its stem and waits for the wind to give it a ride. They can produce up to 100,000 seeds that go flying off as the plant tumbles along.

As far as I know, tumbleweeds are not really good for anything except the annual tumbleweed Christmas tree in Chandler, a pleasantly goofy tradition since 1957.

Navajos Get Most From Retired Tires

January 26, 2002

Today's question: *When I am driving across the Navajo reservation, I always see a lot of old tires hanging on fences or on top of sheds or trailers. What's that about?*

I consulted with my colleague, Betty Reid, for the answer to this one, because she is an actual Navajo person who speaks actual Navajo and actually grew up on the actual Navajo reservation. She is also very nice.

Said she: "Navajos are very practical." This is no doubt true, because Betty always struck me as a fairly practical person.

"Old tires are heavy enough to withstand strong winds and rain, so people use them on a fence for windbreaks or to hold down the roof covers of trailers," she said.

"Sometimes they are cut in half and used as feed bins for livestock or strung together to make a corral. Some people use them to flatten land by dragging them. My father used to burn old tires at night to keep coyotes from nabbing lambs at night."

That sounds reasonable. A burning tire would certainly keep me from nabbing a lamb at night.

Toilet Paper In Colors Is For Sissies

January 27, 2002

You realize, of course, that I should be at home in bed right now, sipping chicken soup or something. I have a head cold. I have the worst head cold anybody ever had. I have the Black Death of head colds, and I want to whine about it. I should probably be cauterized or quartered or whatever you call it. Quarantined. That's it.

Instead I am sitting here in my dimly lit, dank cubicle, a threadbare blanket over my shivering shoulders. I think a rat just ran across my foot.

Plucky lad that I am, I am risking my health to bring you the answers to questions such as this:

We recently moved to the Valley, and we love all the scenery, amenities, and activities the region has to offer. However, one amenity the Valley seems to lack is colored toilet paper. How can we accessorize our home if the only color of toilet paper available is white?

You accessorize your home with toilet paper?

There is a very good reason why you cannot easily find colored toilet paper here: Because we are not a bunch of namby-pamby East Coast wimps. Out West, where, for the most part, men are men and women are women, we like our water bottled, our horns swoggled and our toilet paper white.

I can't believe I actually checked this one out.

According to Dave Dickson, a spokesman for Kimberly-Clark in Dallas, 52 percent of all colored toilet paper is purchased in the northeastern states.

Fifteen percent is purchased in Arizona, Washington, Oregon, California, Utah, Idaho, Montana, Colorado and Wyoming.

In both the Southeast and north central states it's 13 percent, and in the Southwest, mostly Texas and New Mexico, it's just 7 percent. I don't know why they didn't put us in with them, instead of with Oregon, etc. They just did.

Is there a reason for these regional differences? Dickson had a ready answer:

"No."

Good. I'm going home.

When Herons Set Up House, Just Look Out

February 3, 2002

The other day I got a note from a gentleman who had discovered 19 dead fish, some of them partially digested, beside his swimming pool and a great blue heron in his pine tree.

Naturally, he was concerned.

Now me, I like great blue herons. They manage to be gangly and elegant at the same time. Still, this dead fish thing is worrisome. The Brown Cloud is bad enough, not to mention the pigeons. The thought of great blue herons flying around and rolfing up fish all over the backyard is unsettling. You'd certainly want to keep the kiddies inside.

It turned out the gentleman with the dead fish lived about half a mile from a golf course, which of course has some ponds, which of course had fish. And the heron, according to Joe Janisch of the state Game and Fish Department, was just setting up housekeeping.

I have to admit I was somewhat disappointed in this. I was hoping it was a rogue heron, a great blue gone bad.

"This is not unusual," Janisch said. "It's that time of year when they are building nests."

As for the 19 dead fish, the bird either dropped them down through the tree while starting to build a nest or left them by the pool to pick up later. "It's like a refrigerator or a storage area to the bird," Janisch said. "You'll find all sorts of stuff under a heron's nest, partially eaten fish to some that are still flopping."

As I said, I like herons, although I don't know if I'd like one living in my backyard. They tend to gather in colonies, and their nests are not exactly attractive.

The blue heron can stand as tall as 54 inches and have a wingspread of 6 feet. In addition to fish, they eat turtles, frogs, snakes, crawfish, lizards and rodents, so this guy who sent me the note can look forward to finding all sorts of interesting body parts under his tree.

I didn't know this before, but in some parts of the country, herons are called "big crankies," which, if you ask me, is another point in their favor.

Greenway Road Named After A Hero

February 17, 2002

Today's question: *Is Greenway Road named for someone or is the name meant to be descriptive? Most of it doesn't seem very green, although it does have some nice parts.*

Well, even the dullest and drabbest of us do have some nice parts, don't you think?

Greenway Road is named for Gen. John C. Greenway, a World War I hero and mining magnate. There is a statue of him in the old Capitol Building in Washington, D.C.

He was, as noted, a war hero and big shot, but the street could have just as easily have been named for his wife, Isabella S. Greenway, one of the most remarkable women in Arizona history.

She was born in 1886 in Kentucky and grew up wealthy in Manhattan. She was a bridesmaid at the wedding of Franklin Delano Roosevelt and her girlhood friend Eleanor Roosevelt, and gave the seconding speech for FDR at the Democratic National Convention in 1932.

She came West with her first husband, a former Rough Rider named Robert H. Munro Ferguson, who suffered from tuberculosis. He died in 1922, and she married Greenway, an old flame. He died two years later, and Isabella took over his vast business holdings.

In 1935, Greenway was the first Arizona woman elected to Congress, where she served two terms. In Depression-era Congress, she championed issues benefiting mines, ranchers and cotton growers. She also brought three New Deal resettlement projects to the state and pestered the Public Health Service until they came to the aid of 60 transient families camped under the Central Avenue bridge in Phoenix.

Outside the political arena, she was the founder of Tucson's fabled Arizona Inn, owned a huge ranch near Williams, opened a birth control clinic in Tucson over the objections of the Roman Catholic Church, owned a commercial airline and ran a company that employed disabled veterans. She was, in short, no slouch. She died in Tucson in 1953.

East Is East; West Is West; Well, Maybe

February 24, 2002

Today we have two questions from people who aren't quite sure where they are. I am in complete sympathy, because I often am not quite sure where I am. It happens.

Would you please explain the difference between Scottsdale mailing addresses and city limits in the area of Tatum and Shea boulevards and Scottsdale and Bell roads?

And:

What exactly is the East Valley?

The city limits/ZIP code thing gets a bit complicated. The U.S. Postal Service determines addresses and delivers mail by ZIP codes. For the most part, the ZIP boundaries match city limits but not always.

This was explained to me by the extremely helpful Jeanne Herberger, an address management systems specialist for the postal service.

For example, the postal service considers the ZIP 85254 to be a Scottsdale address even though it includes parts of Phoenix. It is bounded by Tatum and Shea boulevards, Scottsdale Road and the Central Arizona Project aqueduct.

If you live in that area, there is a good chance you are a Phoenix resident with a Scottsdale mailing address. Why? Because the U.S. Postal Service says so.

As for the East Valley thing, I'm not sure I want to get into this, because I bet almost everyone has a different idea of what's east and what isn't.

I will tell you this: Wide World of Maps, publisher of the indispensable *Phoenix Metropolitan Street Atlas* that I filched off someone else's desk, offers maps of six Valley areas, including Southeast No. 1 and Southeast No. 2.

The first one includes Tempe, Guadalupe, Chandler, Sun Lakes, Scottsdale south of McDonald Drive, the Arcadia and Papago areas of Phoenix, and Mesa and Gilbert west of Power Road.

Southeast No. 2 includes Apache Junction, Queen Creek, and Mesa and Gilbert east of Lindsay Road.

None of these is around central Phoenix so they are east enough for me.

Pulling Wool Over Our, Er, Rats' Eyes

March 2, 2002

A number of you have called or written in the past week or so to ask why I have not written anything snarky about roof rats and my masters.

I don't know. I guess it just doesn't seem fair to the rats.

So we shall take up today's question without any unseemly comparisons.

The other day in the paper it said roof rats have "large ears that can be pulled over the eyes." Why would a roof rat want to pull its ears over its eyes?

That's a pretty good question. I looked for the answer for some time without success and then polled some of my colleagues to see if they had any ideas. The consensus was that since roof rats are nocturnal and sleep during the day they fold their big ears over their little rat eyes to keep out Mr. Sunshine while they snooze.

You know, some days I think it's a wonder that we get a newspaper out at all.

Anyway, I finally did what I should have done in the first place, which was to call the always helpful Laura Devany, a spokeswoman for Maricopa County Environmental Services, which includes Vector Control. Vector, by the way, in the sense of a pest, comes from the Latin *vectus* meaning a "carrier or bearer." As in a carrier of some loathsome disease.

The charming Ms. Devany went and asked somebody for me and soon reported that roof rats do not pull their ears over their eyes when they sleep. Instead, the matter of whether the ears could cover the eyes is just one means that rat-ologists use to tell one kind of rat from another.

So, for instance, if you had a rat and found that you could not pull its ears over its eyes, you would know it was not a roof rat. It might be a Norway rat, and a very annoyed one at that if you keep tugging at its ears that way.

One last thing: I do not believe my masters can pull their ears over their eyes, although I haven't actually gotten close enough to check.

Harrises Eat Like Birds, So Pooch Is Safe

March 4, 2002

I like this lady's question because she went on to say she asked it because she is still afraid of those flying monkeys from the *Wizard of Oz*. Me, too.

Our back yard backs up to a mountain preserve. About 100 yards from our house is a saguaro with three Harris hawks in residence. We recently adopted a golden retriever puppy that weighs 9 pounds and enjoys sleeping in the grass. I am worried that the hawks will see her as a tasty meal.

You probably don't need to worry, at least not about the hawks.

An adult male Harris weighs between 18 and 26 ounces, while the females weigh up to 30 ounces. They eat desert stuff: mice, lizards, rabbits, quail. Small stuff compared to a puppy.

However, I am told that Harris hawks really hate coyotes and have been known to attack strange dogs that wander into their territories. Even brave dogs are supposedly terrorized by this, and I don't blame them. I would be, too.

Maybe if the hawks hang around while the puppy is growing up, they won't consider it a threat. I don't know.

Harris hawks are very common around here. If you see a hawk, chances are that it's either a Harris or a red tail.

One interesting thing about Harrises is that they are one of only two species that are social hunters. The other is the Galapagos hawk. They live in family groups of two or three generations and hunt by leapfrogging over an area in teams until they find supper.

Like most raptors, they have excellent eyesight, as much as 30 times better than a person with 20/20 vision. They can see a rabbit a mile away.

This is weird: Harris hawks also are known to "stack." If one is perched on top of a saguaro or something, another one might come along and sit on the first one's shoulders. Nobody seems to know why.

Anyway, the puppy is probably OK. On the other hand, I'd keep an eye out for the flying monkeys. They got Toto, didn't they?

Desert Story: Dew Point Can Be Minus

March 8, 2002

Many of you have called or written lately to inquire about the dew point readings, a topic usually reserved for the steamy days of summer.

Specifically, you are concerned, some of you to the point of near hysteria, about a recent spate of negative dew point readings. Soothe yourselves, meine Freunde. All will soon become clear; calm will be restored; and life will continue in all its fullness and wonder.

Let's review: The dew point temperature is the point at which water vapor in the air changes from a gas to water or a solid (dew or frost, depending on the temperature). It has to do with relative humidity and temperature and the fact that the amount of water the air can hold varies with the temperature. This, of course, will be of great concern in a few months when people crank up their evaporative coolers.

As good old David Runyan of the National Weather Service put it, the dew point is a "calculated" temperature as opposed to a "sensed" temperature.

I found a formula for calculating the dew point and, trust me, you don't want to hear about it. It ran for three full lines of type on an 8 ½ by 11 sheet of paper. You don't want to fool around with stuff like that, because under certain atmospheric conditions, it can make your brain explode.

So anyway, yes, it is possible to have a negative dew point, just as it is possible to have a temperature below zero. And that is just what has been happening. The air over the Valley has been so dry lately that humidity readings have fallen as low as 3 percent, and dew points have been as low as minus 9 degrees Fahrenheit.

So if the dew point is minus 9, that means the temperature would have to fall to 9 below zero before the air could not hold any more water and frost would form. Since cold air cannot hold as much water as warm air, that means it's pretty darn dry, which is why my firm yet somehow sensuous lips are all chapped, and my socks dry really fast on the clothesline.

Opossums In Arizona? Sure — Sort Of

April 5, 2002

Today's question: *My wife swears she saw an opossum the other night while walking the dog in our Mesa neighborhood. I think she was seeing things. Settle our bet. Are there opossums in Arizona?*

Are there opossums in Arizona? Are you kidding?

Why do you think some parts of the state are uninhabited? There are opossums out there the size of St. Bernards, mutated by the drift from nuclear testing back in the '50s. Their teeth are as long as car keys, and they are notoriously short-tempered. In 1973, a group of Boy Scouts camping near…

OK, I made that stuff up. I thought it might be more interesting than the real answer, which is: Sort of.

There are opossums in Arizona, although it is highly unlikely that the missus saw one in Mesa. Unlikely, but not impossible.

Arizona's opossum population mostly confines itself to the area from Tucson south to the border. That's fine with me. I think opossums are sort of creepy. I had a teacher once who looked like an opossum. She was creepy, too.

The only things I like about opossums are the names of all the different types — Central American wooly opossum, Alston's mouse opossum, Virginia opossum and my favorite — Gray's four-eyed opossum. I have no idea if it really has four eyes. I doubt it. It's just a cool name.

Anyway, researchers used to think our opossums were ordinary opossums somehow transplanted from the East. (Who would drive an opossum to Arizona?) But it turns out they are a subspecies of Mexican opossums that has moved north and expanded its numbers during the wet years a couple decades ago. Mexican opossums have longer, darker tails than common opossums, in case you were wondering.

In the course of looking stuff up, I also came across some recipes for cooking opossum. As a public service, I will not be printing them here, and you may not call and ask for them. They're enough to make you retch.

A History Of Beeline Highway

April 7, 2002

Today's question: *What is the origin of the name of the Beeline Highway?*

I am indebted for the answer to this question to Doug Nintzel of the state Department of Transportation, who sent me portions of a history of the Beeline written by Payson historian Stan Brown. And also to my pals in the maps section of the state library. They're always very cheerful in the maps section. It must be a cool job.

People have been trying to get to Payson from Phoenix even before there was a Phoenix or a Payson. For centuries, Native American trade routes ran between the two.

Before there was the Beeline, Arizona 87, there was the Bush Highway, and before the Bush there was the Reno Road, which the Army built in the 1860s.

The Bush Highway was the idea of a Mesa lumberman named Harvey Bush who in the early 1930s talked Maricopa County and the U.S. Forest Service into building a new road to the Mogollan Rim.

The road began at Power Road and what is now the Superstition Freeway. When it was completed, you could drive to Payson from the Valley in all of nine hours.

The Bush ran roughly parallel to the Beeline, and if you fly over the area in a helicopter, you can still see parts of the old road, unless you have your eyes squeezed shut tight because you hate helicopters.

No sooner was the Bush finished than people started pushing for its improvement. In the early '50s, a Maricopa County supervisor named Jim Hart, who had a cabin in Payson, persuaded the Salt River Pima and Fort McDowell Yavapai tribes to give up a diagonal right-of-way across their reservations.

That's how the highway got its name. The shortcut made it a beeline to Payson.

The Beeline began at McDowell Road and Country Club Drive, hit the Bush at the turnoff to Saguaro Lake and followed the old highway off and on to Payson. It wasn't paved until 1958.

State Has 2 Natural (Dry) Lakes
April 14, 2002

Today's question: *When my friends in Minnesota ask me how we can have lakes in the desert, I tell them we only have one natural lake and the rest are all manmade. Am I correct in telling them Stoneman Lake is our only natural lake?*

Not quite. Mormon Lake also is a natural lake. There may be some honest-to-goodness ponds or whatever around, but aside from Stoneman and Mormon, all the other lakes in Arizona are manmade. I think there are 67, but I'm not sure if that includes the urban lakes, too.

At the moment, however, Stoneman and Mormon are lakes in name only. The prolonged drought in northern Arizona has left them as dry and shriveled as my masters' souls.

This is unfortunate but not unheard of. Both of them are "wet-weather" lakes, and without rain and snowmelt they dry up.

Mormon Lake is about 25 miles southeast of Flagstaff. It was "discovered" in 1873 by a pair of brothers named Casner, according to *Arizona Place Names*. It got its name from — surprise! — a Mormon colony known as Mormon Dairy that was established there in the 1878.

It's a shame Stoneman Lake is dried up because it is a really pretty place. It's about 40 or so miles south of Flagstaff off of Interstate 17. Spanish explorers first saw it in 1583.

It was once known as Owens Lake, but was later named for Gen. George Stoneman, who crossed Arizona in 1846 with the Mormon Battalion and went on to be governor of California.

They used to think the lake was a meteor crater, but now they think it was formed by a collapse along a fault line in the limestone.

In her 1908 book *Vanishing Arizona*, Martha Summerhayes called Stoneman Lake, "Far and away the most beautiful spot I ever saw in Arizona."

If she thought Arizona was vanishing in 1908, I wonder what she would think about it today.

Dead Stars, Citrus Woes Or Whatever

April 19, 2002

In the course of researching today's question, I came across a swell new Web site or at least a swell Web site that's new to me. It's the Dead People Server, http://dpsinfo.com/dps.html. It tells you which celebrities or other famous people are dead and which ones are alive.

Actually, I didn't find this site while I was researching today's question, but while I was thinking about researching it. I was letting my brain cool off by reading the paper, and I found a story that said Phyllis Diller was retiring from stand-up comedy. I thought Phyllis Diller was dead. It turns out she's 84 and just now retiring. Who knew? No disrespect, mind you. It's perfectly fine with me that Phyllis Diller isn't dead, and I'm sure she is pleased.

Anyway, today's question comes from someone who is apparently new to the Valley or at least new to citrus trees.

Help! *All the little baby oranges are falling off my tree. The ground is covered with little pea-sized green oranges.*

Do not be alarmed, sir or madam. If you were to go outside and find that Phyllis Diller had fallen out of your tree, that would be different. However, in this case, you are witnessing a perfectly normal occurrence known as "green drop" or sometimes "June drop."

Certain kinds of trees, citrus among them, often set more fruit than it is possible for them to sustain and mature. So not long after the tree blooms and the teeny-tiny fruit start to appear, the tree takes stock of things, nutrients, the weather and its age and decides to let some of the fruit go. It is a natural thinning process, just as you as a gardener might thin out a row of newly sprouted arugula, although, if I had arugula in my garden, I would thin it out with a backhoe.

Hot weather and dry wind can cause a heavier than normal drop.

In any event, don't worry. Barring some disaster, your tree will have plenty of fruit next winter.

Meanwhile, while you may be saddened to know that Roddy McDowall has joined the Choir Invisible, Abe Vigoda lives.

These 'Toads' Are Losing Their Habitat

April 21, 2002

Today's question: *When I was a kid growing up in Phoenix there used to be horny toads everywhere. I even had a pet horny toad. Now I never see them. What happened to all the horny toads?*

You had a pet horny toad? That's sad. Couldn't you get your parents to buy you a dog or a cat or a goldfish or something?

Let's start with the most important part of this matter: If you want to hear Yosemite Sam say "Great horny toads!" go to this site: http://uts.cc.utexas.edu/~iffp475/phrynoshtml/HHT.html.

Now, for one thing, horny toads are not really toads. They are horned lizards. There are 14 species of these beasties in North and South America, eight in the United States. They are distinguished by 30 to 35 spines of varying lengths around the head and neck.

They are about as Arizonan as you can get. Almost every ancient Native American culture — Anasazi, Hohokam, Mogollon — recorded horny toads in pottery or petroglyphs.

I consulted with Glenn Walsberg, professor of biology at Arizona State University, on the matter of the scarcity of horny toads, and he said it probably is a loss of habitat.

Horny toads are not particularly urban creatures. Desert, dirt roads, farm fields — that's where you find horny toads. Look out the window. See any desert, dirt roads or farm fields? See any horny toads?

Another possibility, I suppose, is the fact that horny toads eat ants, and over the years we have been infested with Argentine ants. Maybe horny toads don't like Argentine ants. I don't know.

One thing about horny toads: When threatened by a predator they can squirt blood out of their eyes from a special sinus behind their eyeballs. This is pretty cool. Not even my masters would eat something that had blood squirting out of its eyeballs, although you can never tell about them.

How Many Chiropractors Does It Take?

April 28, 2002

I get a lot of good questions from snowbirds. It's like what they say about cats: They see things we don't.

Today's question, for example, is from a guy from Maine.

How many chiropractors does it take to heal an Arizonan? It seems like I see chiropractic offices on every corner in the Valley. Why are there so many?

You know, it never occurred to me that there were a lot of chiropractors around here. I just never noticed.

Anyway, for the answer I turned to my old pal Patty Pritzel, who is the director of the state Board of Chiropractic Examiners. I didn't even know she was my old pal, until she reminded me, because I hadn't seen her in a long time. I didn't even know she was the director of the state Board of Chiropractic Examiners and, by golly, there she was examining chiropractors.

It turns out the guy from Maine was right. You can't swing a cat around here without hitting a chiropractor. We have more of them per capita than any other state: one for every 1,480 people. Florida is next with one chiropractor for every 1,860 people. Who knew?

Whence this clutter of chiros?

For one thing, Pritzel said, chiropractors come here for the same reasons the rest of us did: the weather, the opportunities, the beautiful Southwest.

For another, licensing fees here are only $200, compared with $400 or $500 in other states. That's changing, she said. The fees will soon go up to $350.

And we obviously have a lot of older people around here, and Pritzel said, "Older people tend to have more of the kinds of problems chiropractors treat."

Furthermore, *The Republic's* health maven, Jodie Snyder, pointed out that many forms of alternative medicine are big in Arizona and that chiropractic might be considered the grandfather of alternative medicine. You could say chiropractic is the backbone of alternative medicine. Backbone. Get it? Ha! That was a good one.

Thick Water May Impede Care Of Pool

May 5, 2002

Today, because it is the season for such matters, we are going to discuss swimming pools.

If you already know everything there is to know about swimming pools or if you do not have a pool or if you do not like swimming pools, perhaps you would like to move on to something else. Or you can stick around in case I try to sneak in a dirty joke. It's up to you.

Why does it seem easier for me to brush down the sides of my pool when it is warm than it is when it's cold? Maybe the bristles of the brush aren't as stiff in warm weather?

Hmmm, this could get a little tricky. As water cools it becomes denser until it hits about 39 degrees or so and then actually becomes less dense, which is why ice floats. The ice part doesn't have anything to do with the question, though.

Lower temperatures also increase the viscosity of water. It would, for example, take about twice as much energy to row a boat in water that was nearly freezing than it would be row on a sunny, summer day.

In theory, the greater density and viscosity could account for the extra brushing effort. However, I'm thinking that since a pool is so small and since the effort involved in brushing the sides is not exactly Herculean, colder temperatures shouldn't really make that much difference. So maybe it's your imagination.

This may come as a shock to you, but I could be wrong about that.

Bees are always drowning in my pool. Why don't they learn to avoid it?

Because they have little, teeny-tiny bee brains, that's why. They're not programmed to learn lessons like that.

About the only way to keep bees out of the pool is to switch from chlorine to a salt water sanitation system. Bees hate saltwater.

There are oval-shaped bugs in our pool. They swim, and we think they bite. When we throw them out they crawl and hop back toward the pool. What are they?

I don't know.

Saguaros Store Their Own Water

May 15, 2002

Today's question: *Why are there such spectacular blossoms on the saguaros this year if we are in a big drought?*

I have had to admit this before and do so again now: It's a good thing I have you people around — or at least some of you people — to remind me about stuff.

Just last week I went down to Tucson on the interstate and home the back way through Florence, and I saw a lot of saguaros in huge blossom, but it didn't dawn on me to wonder about this until I got this question.

I probably was preoccupied thinking of questions about gigantic hairy bugs or atomic frogs or the such.

Anyway, this one's easy. Patrick Quirk, the always-helpful cactus expert at the Desert Botanical Garden, pointed out that saguaros store their own water, so they can put on the dog — blossom-wise — drought or not.

But it's not just the cactus. Kim Stone, a horticulturist at the Boyce Thompson Arboretum near Superior, said he can't remember when he has seen the ironwoods and blue paloverdes in such full flower. However, he said, while there may be a lot of flowers, those plants aren't putting out many leaves, probably because of the drought.

Here's an idea that both Stone and Quirk tossed out: In times of drought, it is possible that some plants produce more blossoms, and hence more seeds, in an effort to increase their chances of reproducing and spreading their progeny. It's like just in case, as Quirk said, this is the "ultimate drought."

Ultimate drought — sounds kind of creepy, doesn't it?

Like maybe the ironwoods and paloverdes know something we don't?

Both Stone and Quirk said the extra-production-during-drought thing was only an idea and couldn't prove it.

I think they thought I was actually going to do the extra work involved in tracking it down 10 minutes before the Cubs game started.

Shaa.

Don't Get Tangled Up In The Web
June 6, 2002

I get a lot of questions about hummingbirds, which is fine because I like hummingbirds. And they keep the cat entertained without injury to themselves, which is more than I can do.

This is a hummingbird question I get a lot:

How do I keep finches away from my hummingbird feeder?

Try using those little yellow bee guards and removing any perches from the feeder. Or just don't worry about it. The hummingbirds will still get their share, and sugar water is cheap.

That, however, is not the hummingbird issue at hand today. This is:

Once I found a baby hummingbird caught in a black widow spider's web. I cut it free with nail scissors and put it back in the nest and later I saw it fly away again. I've always wondered if the black widow spider would have killed the baby hummingbird if I had not cut it free.

Deader than a doornail.

Which were not the exact words of Carol Crosswhite, the curator of zoology at the Boyce Thompson Arboretum near Superior, but it was pretty much what she said.

Black widow spiders, as you surely know, are very nasty little things. The black widow's venom is a neurotoxin that stuns its prey into sort of a coma. Then the black widow sucks out all the juices.

Anyway, Crosswhite said, yes, the black widow probably would have bitten the baby hummingbird. "It was something wiggling in the web, and black widows are programmed to bite things that are wiggling in the web." And the venom probably would have been enough to put the bird in a coma.

However, black widows are not programmed to eat things that big, so it probably would not have tried to suck out all the juices. So I suppose the bird would have died of shock or exposure.

Let's try in the future to ask questions that don't involve things sucking all the juices out of other things, shall we?

Cloud-Seed Suggestion Is All Wet

June 8, 2002

Here's a question that has been coming in a lot lately:

If the drought is so bad, why don't we seed the clouds to make it rain?

For the same reason we don't go around hopping up and down on one foot and yelling, "Booga, booga, booga." It would be silly.

You people.

I put this matter to the Salt River Project, and spokesman Jeff Lane said, "The simple answer is that there aren't more clouds. You can't seed clouds that aren't there, and Arizona has more sunshine than any other state."

This is not to say the matter hasn't been experimented with around the state. In the past, the U.S. Bureau of Reclamation and some other agencies have looked at various cloud-seeding tests, but nothing much ever came of them. You can find a pretty good report on this at http://ag.arizona.edu/AZWATER. Click on "publications" and then on "arroyo."

Clouds are made of supercooled water droplets that eventually form ice crystals around little bits of dust or other particulates. When they get heavy enough, it rains. Cloud-seeding works by adding some kind of particles — silver iodide or dry ice — to give the droplets more stuff to glom on to and form ice crystals. If there are no supercooled water droplets there to begin with, there's nothing to seed.

Even if it were feasible, there is a lot of stuff about cloud seeding they haven't figured out yet. The environmental impacts are not always clear. Who should pay for it? Where is it actually going to rain? Let's say, just hypothetically, that SRP seeded the clouds over the Mogollon Rim, and it worked so well that it caused heavy flooding. Who is liable for the damage? What if California seeded a cloud mass that was headed for us so they got rain and we didn't? Did they steal our rain?

Sorry, you'll have to come up with a new plan. Let me know. On second thought, don't.

Cockroaches Don't Always Die Feet Up

June 12, 2002

Today we have a frequently asked question about cockroaches.

However, first I have to say that the last time I wrote about cockroaches, a number of you called or wrote and allowed as how cockroaches, especially headless cockroaches or microwaved cockroaches, were not the sort of thing you cared to read about while taking in your recommended daily allowance of Froot Loops.

Well, it can't be helped. This is a morning paper, after all.

Maybe you should skip to the funnies until you're done eating and then come back.

Speaking of that, I met a guy the other day who said the trouble with the funnies is they have "too many words" in them.

Too many words in the funnies.

I put my head down on the desk and sighed for a while.

Anyway, the question:

Why do cockroaches always die on their backs with their feet up in the air?

For one thing, they don't always die on their backs.

For example, if a cockroach is crawling along and all of the sudden it has a stroke or a heart attack or it gets whopped with a shoe, it would likely die in its tracks, its back up.

I did put this matter to Dawn Gouge, an entomologist at the University of Arizona's Maricopa Agriculture Center and a very nice person.

She said a cockroach's hard exoskeleton makes it kind of back-heavy, if you will.

So, if a cockroach gets poisoned or gassed or is inflicted with a case of the vapors or attacked by some kind of neurotoxin, it might go into convulsions and start flailing its disgusting roach legs around and all that convulsing and flailing would cause it to flip on its back, and it probably would be unable to right itself before joining the roach choir invisible.

Try it yourself sometime and see if that doesn't happen to you. OK?

So that's the answer.

I just hope there aren't too many words in it.

State Flag's Tale Not Too Surprising

June 14, 2002

Today is Flag Day, and as luck would have it, I have at hand an honest-to-goodness flag question. Actually, I have two flag questions, but I can't find the answer to one of them. I may throw that one out for you guys to answer, but not today.

As a young boy growing up in Texas, I was taught in school the location of Texas' star in the blue field of the U.S. flag. What's the location of Arizona's star?

I didn't even know until this question came in that each state had a designated star on the flag, but apparently they do. Seems a bit much to me, but I guess there's no harm in it.

It turns out the placement of the states' stars on the flag is determined by the order of their admittance to the Union.

Delaware, the first state to ratify the Constitution, is the star in the upper left-hand corner, and Pennsylvania, the second state in, is to the right of that, and so on.

Arizona's star is in the bottom row, the third one in from the right.

While we're on the subject of flags, did you know Arizona didn't come up with a state flag until five years after statehood was granted? It took the Legislature that long to agree on a design.

The design finally adopted was by Charles W. Harris. The 13 red and gold rays on the top half represent the original 13 colonies, and the rays of the setting sun.

The big star is meant to represent the state's copper industry. The blue in the bottom half is the same blue as in the U.S. flag and is meant to represent…umm, blue, I guess.

Anyway, a lot of people hated it at first because they thought it looked too much like Japan's rising-sun flag. The same thing came up during World War II.

Gov. Thomas Campbell hated the design so much that he let the bill creating the flag become law without his signature in 1917.

Five years of legislative bickering over a seemingly minor issue. Why does that not seem surprising?

Query Sows The Seeds Of Knowledge

June 23, 2002

Today's question: *We are new to the area, so perhaps everyone around here knows the answer to this except us. We have discovered when we water most of the low plants and bushes in our yard, we hear an audible pop or crackling sound, one every few seconds. What is that and what causes it?*

You're right, everyone around here knows about this except you.

Even now, all over the Valley, longtime residents are throwing down their newspapers and laughing uproariously at your newcomer foolishness. They are saying to their spouses, "Hey, Marge, can you believe these people didn't know about the popping sound thing? These wacky newcomers, what are we going to do with them?"

This only confuses their spouses because they are not named Marge.

Actually, I had never heard of this before, and neither had anyone else until I finally asked Cathy Rymer at the Cooperative Extension Service. They know everything at the Cooperative Extension Service. Lose your car keys? Call the Extension Service; they'll know where they are.

The questioner did not specify what sort of plants he is watering that make a popping sound, but Rymer said it is more than likely ruellia, *Ruellia brittoniana*, more commonly known as Mexican petunia. It usually has a tall stalk with bright purple, tubular leaves, but the dwarf version is often used as a ground cover.

The thing about ruellia, according to Rymer, is that when it gets wet, its seedpods explode with an audible pop and send the seeds flying every which way. And so many seeds can go whizzing around that it sometimes sounds like rain.

That's kind of interesting, don't you think?

So, you see, it's not a matter of everybody knowing this except newcomers. I'm just glad they didn't ask about the you-know-what. You have to be here two years before we can tell you about that.

Evaporative Cooler Saves Your Money

July 7, 2002

Today we have an evaporative cooler doubleheader, two related questions that I shall try to answer as if I actually knew what I was talking about.

And since, of course, I don't actually know what I am talking about, I am indebted to Tom Babcock, a water resources specialist for the city of Phoenix, for help on both these matters.

I know I am saving a ton on my utility bill by using my evaporative cooler instead of the air-conditioning, but what is this doing to my water bill? And am I wasting water by constantly running it through the cooler?

And:

My pool is losing lots of water to evaporation. So I opened up the bleed on my swamp cooler, and I run the bleed water into the pool. Will I get Legionnaires' disease or hurt my pool by doing this?

First things first. Depending on the size and type of evaporative cooler you have, Babcock said it probably raises your water bill about $10 to $15 a month. That's not bad, considering how much it costs to run your air-conditioner.

You could reduce the amount of water your cooler uses by closing off the bleed valve and just using the same water over and over again. However, you'll ruin your cooler after a couple of years by doing this because it will get clogged up with salts and other solids from the water.

So, what to do about the bleed water dripping off your roof?

Babcock said running it into the pool is not a particularly good idea because it's very high in dissolved solids, calcium, magnesium, sodium chloride, stuff like that. The bleeder water probably won't actually hurt you, but chances are it is not going to do your pool any good.

A better idea would be to hook up a hose and use the bleeder water to irrigate your plants, especially those plants that are salt-tolerant. That way you can brag to your friends who don't have evap about the money you are saving and at the same time be smug about recycling water.

Dust Travels From Afar On Swift Wind

July 16, 2002

Did you see all the back-to-school ads in Sunday's paper? It was full of them. Well, I'm not going back, and they can't make me. I don't care what they say. I did my time.

Besides, I don't need to go back because I know a lot of people who are in school, so if I need to know something I can always ask one of them. Like good old Randy Cerveny at Arizona State University. He knows lots of stuff, which is why I asked him for help on today's question.

The other day after a big windstorm, I was cleaning the cartridges in the pool filter, and I found that the dust was a deep red color, much redder than anything I've seen around here. Has anyone ever researched how far dust and debris can travel in a really good monsoon?

For what it's worth, this question came in before Sunday night's big storm. Was that great or what? Did you dance around naked in the rain in your back yard? Neither did I. It upsets the neighbors and frightens the cat.

Anyway, about the dust in the pool filter:

Wind, according to good old Randy Cerveny, is a very efficient mover of things that can be moved by the wind, especially dust that gets pulled up into the upper levels of the atmosphere where the wind can really clip along.

During this time of year, the monsoon, it is very likely that the dust in the pool filter came from Mexico, Cerveny said, and it is quite reasonable that it would be deep red.

However, we have in the past been powdered with far more exotic imported dust, dust from as far away as China. Last year a huge dust storm in the Gobi Desert blew enough grit across the Pacific Ocean to cause some hazy days in the Phoenix area.

The Gobi seems to be an especially dusty desert, partially because it has a lot of loess, or dust laid down by the wind in the first place, and partially because the area has been in a prolonged drought for some time.

Mesquite Seeds Need Water Only

July 19, 2002

Did you see where they spelled my name wrong in the Valley 101 logo on Wednesday? I haven't felt so much a part of *The Republic* team since they took away my company cell phone because I was deemed "non-essential."

However, that is not the topic at hand. The topic at hand is flying bathtubs. Monday we reported that during the big storm, the wind picked up a bathtub it found somewhere and sent it crashing down in the middle of a street in central Phoenix.

I would have paid to see that. I wonder if someone could organize a bathtub-dropping exhibition and throw a bathtub off a tall building or something like that. I'd go to see that. I'd go twice.

I would organize this myself, but I am far too busy with questions such as this:

I'd like to plant some mesquite, but I've heard they sprout best after passing through the alimentary canal of a bird or a cow or some other animal. Without such an animal, will they still sprout?

Did you know they used to use mesquite wood to pave streets in some towns in Texas? That would be something to see, although still not as cool as the flying bathtub thing.

Yes, it is true that mesquite is dispersed by animals eating the seedpods and depositing the seeds elsewhere. And it is true that such seeds germinate easily because they hit the ground with a big dollop of fertilizer.

However, you do not have to have a cow or a bird or whatever around to grow mesquite. According to Judy Curtis of the Maricopa County Cooperative Extension, you can grow mesquite from fresh or dried beans, but it helps if you soak them in water overnight before planting.

The thing to remember is that mesquite quickly puts down a long taproot, so if you're planting them in a pot, it has to be good and deep. A 3-inch mesquite seedling will have a taproot 8 or 10 inches long. If you're going to transplant them, do it as soon as the first leaves appear. Use some chicken wire to protect it from birds. Or from falling bathtubs.

When It Is Party Time For Toads
July 20, 2002

I have here a question from a reader who wants to know if it is true that at the time of his death John Wayne's colon weighed 65 pounds. Really.

I do not even care to think about John Wayne's colon, much less research it.

Instead, we shall take up a more tasteful matter, toads.

The other night after it rained, I started to hear what sounded like quacking resonating in the night. It was toads running about, croaking, hopping and getting squished by cars.

I want to know about these toads that live underground for years and only come out after a good rain. Why don't they just dry up underground?

Well, if they dried up underground, we wouldn't have any toads, would we? It would be a toad-al loss. Get it? Toad-al? That was a good one.

Arizona has nine species of toads, including the Sonoran desert toad, the great big one that can make your dog sick and supposedly can get you high if you lick it, but then what kind of moron would lick a toad?

Toads can live 10 years or longer if they don't get squished by a car or eaten by something else.

They spend most of that time underground in burrows, often in the beds of temporary ponds that dry up after the rainy season.

You have to figure that living in a burrow eight or nine months out of the year is pretty boring, but then they're toads, aren't they? They probably don't have a lot of expectations.

When the summer rains come, the moisture level in the soil tells the toads it's party time, and they emerge to hop around, croak, mate and eat, mostly around a pond or your swimming pool and mostly at night.

In addition to being sex-crazed, they are big eaters because they have to store up enough fat in the short rainy season to have food and moisture during their hibernation.

While they're out and about, female toads lay up to 8,000 eggs, which hatch and reach maturity in two to eight weeks.

Everyone is in a hurry because they have to get all this done before the rains stop, and it's time to go underground again.

Don't Risk Falling In Big Ditch

July 21, 2002

Today's question: *Why is it that you can walk or jog or ride your bike along all the canals around town except the Central Arizona Project canal? It looks like it would be great for bicycling, but it's all fenced off.*

Simple. They don't want you to fall in. You would probably drown.

Of course, you could just as easily fall in one of the other canals around town, but the CAP aqueduct is a little trickier.

Bob Barrett, a CAP spokesman, said the aqueduct is 80 feet across and 25 feet deep. On any given day, the water is 16 to 18 feet deep.

"It's moving at 4 mph, and it's cold. If you go in, you're going to have trouble getting out," he said.

There are other dangers involved. Along the Salt River Project canals, the water flows over the gates. On the CAP canal, the water flows under the gates. That means if you fell in and missed one of the ladders, you're going to get sucked under the gate and chances are you're not going to come shooting out the other side.

Then there are places like the siphon that runs under the bed of the Agua Fria River. It's 2 miles long. That, as Barrett noted, is a long time to hold your breath.

Were you here when they built the CAP? It's 336 miles long — all fenced, with gates for wildlife — and it runs from Lake Havasu to just south of Tucson. It took 20 years to build, was finished in 1993, and cost $4 billion.

It was built to deliver Arizona's share of Colorado River water to Maricopa, Pinal and Pima counties and moves about 1.5 million acre-feet of water a year.

Here's another good reason to stay out of the aqueduct. It's a big part of the Valley's drinking water supply. Of course, it gets treated before it gets to you, but still you don't want bodies floating around in it, do you then?

If you want to know more about it, the CAP has a swell Web site: www.cap-az.com.

Rhino Beetles Are Unique To This State

July 28, 2002

Today's question: *I have lived here all of my 32 years, and ever since I can remember, every summer at night, I see the biggest, ugliest and fiercest-looking brown beetle. The other night I saw one of these things and sprayed it with bug killer, which only seemed to disorient it. It took undiluted tick poison to kill it. What are these things?*

You know, if I were rich, I would just buy you people bug books and let you figure these things out by yourselves.

I usually just throw away the bug questions because they are usually pretty vague. Along the lines of "I saw a black bug. What was it?"

However, in this case, I'm just about 100 percent sure that this guy saw — and needlessly slaughtered — a rhinoceros beetle, *Dynastes granti*.

They are the largest North American beetles and are believed to be found only in Arizona.

Like my masters, these things are pretty creepy, especially when they're flying. And they hiss by rubbing their abdomen and wing covers together. The beetles, not my masters. My masters hiss the same way other people do.

Unlike my masters, rhinoceros beetles are not at all dangerous. Some people keep them as pets, although they are as ugly as the day is long.

They're usually brown, about 3.5 inches long, and the males have a big pair of horns protruding from their heads. They use them to fight with other males over babes.

The females lay eggs in decaying vegetable matter or stuff like that. When the larva is grown, it makes itself a little hole in the ground and lines it with feces, which dry and form a waterproof coating. The adults dig their way to the surface in a few weeks.

As noted, they are harmless, so there is no need to go dousing them with tick poison or whatever. You people.

They eat tree sap, although I'm told that people who keep them as pets give them peeled fruit and watered-down maple syrup.

The downside to the pet thing is that they only live about a year as adults. However, just like my masters, they breed easily in captivity.

Dust Devils Take Hot Air For A Spin

July 30, 2002

Did you know that last summer some scientists from the University of Arizona did a big study of dust devils near Eloy as part of the planning for exploration of Mars?

I don't know if this should make you feel better about living in Arizona or not. On one hand, we have a fine, cutting-edge institution like UA leading us into new frontiers in space. On the other hand, Arizona is the closest thing to Mars as they could find.

This all came up while I was looking up the answer to today's question.

Has anyone ever measured the wind speed of dust devils?

I thought this was a silly question at first, because dust devils come and go so quickly that you wouldn't be able to test the wind speed. However, I found several sources that said dust devils could hit 50 mph as well as a reference to a dust devil that busted up the Coconino County Fairgrounds in September 2000 with winds estimated at 75 mph.

Who knew?

Dust devils are caused by surface heating, and they often spring up at the edge of two different types of surfaces, like between a patch of irrigated field and raw desert.

This is how it works: The sun heats up the surface so the ground temperature is a lot warmer than the air just above the surface. The hotter air at the surface is less dense and lighter than the air above it, and it goes shooting up through the cooler air. This causes air to flow horizontally inward and the rising hot air starts to rotate. If it is stretched vertically, the rotation picks up speed. It's like a spinning ice skater pulling her arms in toward her body to spin faster. The meteorological term for this is "conservation of angular momentum." Write that down.

As the pocket of hot air rises, it begins to cool and falls through the inside of the vortex. Meanwhile, more hot air is being pulled in and rushes up the outside of the vortex. If the balance is right, the dust devil goes shooting off along the ground and keeps going until it runs out of hot, unstable air to fuel it.

Parenting Of Quail Is A Group Call
July 31, 2002

There is now some thought that the big, ugly rhinoceros beetle in Sunday's column was not a rhinoceros beetle, but was instead a paloverde root borer, which also is big and ugly.

Suits me.

The paloverde root borer, as you may have guessed, bores into paloverde trees, specifically the roots. It also bores into other kinds of trees. They are very active this time of year, especially in the early evening hours.

The paloverde root borer does not, as far as I know, have anything to do with baby quail, which are the subject of two questions today.

When I watch the quail in my back yard, I've noticed the little ones don't seem to be attached to a parent. Are baby quail raised by a parent or by the whole group?

Both, according to Mike Rabe, who is a small-game biologist for the state Game and Fish Department and a hale-fellow-well-met.

For the first week or 10 days or so of a chick's life, the mother quail is on it "like Velcro," Rabe said. After that, he said, the young quail are part of the larger group, "albeit the slow, dumb part of the group. They get killed a lot."

I put out cracked corn for the quail that live in my neighborhood. Can baby quail eat cracked corn? Will it hurt them?

Baby quail eat almost nothing but bugs for the first days, but after that, cracked corn would suit them just fine.

I know it's cool to watch the quail in your back yard, but you really ought to think through this feeding thing. It's not like they're going to clean up every crumb, and pretty soon you'll have other creatures — wood rats, pack rats, rabbits — showing up for the leftovers, and they'll be followed by javelina or coyotes or even bobcats, and the next thing you know, little Fluffy the kitty will have assumed a new role in the food chain.

Actually, I've never seen a bobcat in the wild. That would be pretty cool, but I don't think I'd want to find one in the back yard.

I would quail at the thought.

Folks, Those Doves Aren't Squeaking

August 15, 2002

Did you know that they've figured out that dogs can count and are generally smarter than we give them credit for? You could have fooled me.

They think the ability to count had something to do with making sure all the members of the pack were present and accounted for. I read a story about this the other day and printed it out, and now I can't find it. It'll turn up one of these days.

In the meantime, we shall take up a question about the ubiquitous mourning dove.

Why do doves squeak when they take off? Is it an alarm call? They seem to do it even if there is no obvious sign that something frightened them.

They're not squeaking, you big silly. Mostly the only vocalizing mourning doves do is different variations on "coo."

The "squeaking" you hear is the distinctive whistle of their wings. Mourning doves are built for speed and have long, streamlined wings. The whistle is produced by the sharp flow of air over their wings during takeoff. When doves are frightened, they leap into the air, throwing their wings up and bringing them down with explosive force. At the same time, they spread and tilt their tails at different angles to get a zigzag flight.

Squeaking. For heaven's sake. Sometimes I wonder what would become of you people if you didn't have me to explain things to you.

Anyway, mourning doves belong to the order Columbiformes, which mostly includes a lot of other doves and pigeons. The interesting thing about Columbiformes is that they are the only birds that are able to drink water in one continuous draft, like a horse does. I didn't know that.

They also produce "pigeon milk," which is a mixture of cells and fluids produced in the bird's crop and regurgitated to feed the hatchlings.

Some people hunt doves, and dove breasts are said to be quite tasty, especially when marinated in milk and cooked with mushroom soup. I don't hold much with shooting doves, but if other people do, it's none of my business. I don't think my masters shoot doves, but it sounds like the kind of thing they'd do. You know what I mean?

Arizona Places Named For Blood, Bees

August 16, 2002

One of my favorite reference books is *Arizona Place Names* by Will C. Barnes. It's just full of stuff, and I use it all the time. However, it was only the other day when I was looking up something else that I discovered it includes several pages of Arizona "firsts."

For instance, the first sewing machine in Arizona was imported in either 1864 or 1865 by C.O. Brown, a prosperous Tucson saloon-keeper. Who knew? People came from all around to see it. Brown also brought in the first baby buggy ever seen in Arizona.

Anyway, like I said, I came across this when I was looking up something else, the answers to today's question:

My husband and I travel often between Prescott Valley and Phoenix, and I am wondering about the origin of the names of Crown King, Bumble Bee and Bloody Basin.

Remember the "Name the Fictional Arizona Town Contest" we had awhile back? I still feel kind of bad about that because so many of you hated the winning entry, Shoot First. In retrospect, we should have gone with Lurking Dread, which I liked a lot but my masters felt was "too Californian."

That's neither here nor there. It's just that Bloody Basin is such a great Arizona name, don't you think? Bloody Basin is in the far southeast corner of Yavapai County. According to Barnes, it was named for the many bloody battles with Indians that took place in the area.

Bumble Bee was a stagecoach stop sometimes known as Snider's Station for the man who first operated it. By 1880 it was known as Bumble Bee, named for Bumble Bee Creek, which in turn was named by some prospectors who in 1863 discovered a large bee's nest nearby and got stung while trying to raid it for honey.

Last but not least, Crown King, which was at the end of a branch rail line about 55 miles from Prescott. It was named for the Crown King Mine, which was a big deal there for a while between the late 1880s and early 1900s. It's a nice place to go for a day trip out of the Valley, but be careful because the roads into it tend to be kind of rough.

For Quail, Drought Brings A Dry Spell

August 27, 2002

We have a question today that is actually pretty cool. I know this because it struck me as pretty cool when it came in, and when I called Mike Rabe at the state Game and Fish Department to ask him about it he said, "This is actually a pretty cool question."

Also, it involves the phrase "gonadal development."

The question comes from an observant gentleman in Scottsdale who says:

I've noticed that the quail didn't have as many hatchlings this year, and I understand it is because of the drought. But how do the quail know not to lay as many eggs?

See? Don't you think that's a pretty cool question? What internal switch does the drought throw in quail that tells them not to have as many young?

It's vitamin A, according to Rabe, who is a small-game biologist and knows all about this stuff.

Quail need vitamin A for normal "gonadal development," he said — for healthy reproductive organs. And they get vitamin A from fresh green plants.

Without the usual winter rains, there is not enough moisture in the soil to green up the desert in the spring when the thoughts of quail, such as they are, turn to love.

Without the vitamin A they get from green plants, the quails' reproductive organs do not develop or do not develop fully, so sperm and egg counts are low. They either don't reproduce at all, or they lay fewer fertile eggs.

So there are fewer mouths to feed at a time when there is less food to go around.

The same idea applies to many other animals, Rabe said, and if it's not specifically vitamin A that's missing, it is some other nutritional deficiency. Mule deer, for example, are very quick to adjust their birth rates based on how much vegetation is available.

Don't you think it's kind of interesting that things work out like that?

Rabe said things are so hard for the birds this year that quail densities are probably actually higher in urban areas, where they can find food and water, than in their natural desert habitats.

Saguaros Refuse To Tell Their Ages

September 15, 2002

Today's question is about the saguaro, so those of who you have lived in Arizona for more than a few years are free to talk quietly among yourselves or put your heads down on your desks and rest a bit.

The rest of you, the newcomers, should pay careful attention because, like indicting a governor or driving badly, few things are more purely Arizonan than the saguaro, the bloom of which, after all, is our official state flower.

I've never quite understood why states need official state stuff, like official butterflies or official trees or official bugs. Would a major corporation be less likely to move here if our state bird were the roadrunner instead of the cactus wren? I suppose there's no harm in it; I just don't get the point.

Today's question: *You can tell how old a tree is by counting its rings. How do you determine the age of a saguaro?*

"You don't," according to the inestimable Patrick Quirk of the Desert Botanical Garden in Phoenix.

Saguaros don't have growth rings, so "there is no reliable way to date their age except in a very broad range," Quirk said. "A saguaro in Tucson might be twice as big as one in Yuma but the same age."

You could make a few good guesses at the age of saguaro, but mostly everything depends on growing conditions. The cactus in Tucson would get a lot more rain than the one in Yuma.

Saguaros, as even you newcomers must know, grow very, very slowly and can live to be 200 years old or older.

But I didn't know this about them. I found it on the Arizona Sonora Desert Museum's Web site. It turns out that saguaros, which we think of as eternal symbols of the desert, are relative newcomers to the area. For about 10,000 years, since the last ice age, they have been expanding their range into these parts.

The fossil record shows that saguaros didn't hit the Tucson area until about 8,000 years ago, which means there were people in the area before there were saguaros. That's kind of interesting, don't you think?

'Diamond Fields' Devoid Of Such
October 20, 2002

Today's question: *I have an 1891 map that shows an area in northeastern Arizona as "Diamond Fields." Have diamonds been found in this area, and if so, are diamonds mined there now?*

This turned out to be pretty interesting. There is indeed a wide spot on the road near the junction of U.S. 160 and Arizona 118 called Diamond Fields.

For help on this matter I called the Old Scout himself, state historian Marshall Trimble, and asked him if he had ever heard of Diamond Fields. That was dumb. Of course he'd heard of Diamond Fields. That's why he's the state historian, and you and I aren't.

In 1872, a pair of prospectors named Philip Arnold and John Slack walked into a bank in San Francisco with a bag full of diamonds and rubies and other gems they had found at a site that they refused to divulge.

They were, of course, crooks, and the gems were industrial-grade stuff they had picked somewhere.

Nonetheless, they conned a pack of investors into setting up a $10 million syndicate in what became known as the Great Diamond Hoax.

You have to remember, as Trimble pointed out, that this was a time when folks thought you could find gold in any coyote hole in the West. A brochure for one mining scheme at the time showed an ocean-going ore ship steaming up the Hassayampa River, Trimble said.

The hoax is a long and colorful story, but it comes down to this: When pressed for details, Arnold and Slack led a blindfolded representative of the investors to a site in southern Colorado they had "salted" with their low-grade gems. The plot was eventually undone by Clarence King of the U.S. Geological Survey who found the site and quickly spotted the hoax. Arnold and Slack skipped town with $155,000.

In the meantime, however, diamond fever was sweeping the West, and prospectors were scouring the land looking for Arnold and Slack's bonanza. One focus of the search was in far northeastern Arizona where, of course, there were no diamonds, but there is still Diamond Fields.

Tiny Creatures From The Stock Tank

October 22, 2002

Today's question: *My husband and kids were out hiking and stopped at a stock tank to look for animal tracks. In the water, they saw these amazing prehistoric bug-looking things. They have a horseshoe-shaped shell with what looks like eyes on it. From under the open end of the shell, there is a tail with a forked end. When you flip them over, they have a dark-orange fringe that looks like millipede legs. What is it?*

Ooo. Ooo. Ask me. Ask me. I know this one. Ask me. I am soooo smart.

I actually did know this one, but just to be sure, I doubled-checked in my handy *Insects of the Southwest* by good old Floyd Werner and good old Carl Olson. What these people found in the stock tank was one of the desert's most interesting creatures: tadpole shrimp.

Crustaceans in the desert. Who would have thought of that? Isn't that great?

Tadpole shrimp, and their cousins fairy shrimp, are not especially closely related to honest-to-goodness shrimp, and in the fossil record, they appeared about 100 million years before shrimp. In fact, they were here before the dinosaurs.

Tadpole shrimp live in stock tanks or desert waterholes. Their eggs can remain viable for a long time if the tank or waterhole dries up. When the water returns, tadpole shrimp hatch, develop, eat a lot, mate, lay more eggs, generally tear up the pea patch and then die in a space of about 30 or 40 days.

They thrive in the mud at the bottom of a tank or pond, which they churn up as they feed on the microorganisms they find there. They have very sturdy jaws and will eat plants and animals, and sometimes each other.

Fairy shrimp are much smaller, and you can almost see through them. Females have a bulge in their middles, the egg sac. Also, they swim upside down. I don't know why.

So if they are so tiny and only live a few weeks in the confines of a pond or tank, how is it that they are so widespread? I'm glad you asked.

It's because their little teeny-tiny eggs get carried from place to place on the mud sticking to the feet of birds. Cool.

Here's The Full Monty On Nelson
November 11, 2002

So the other day this guy from Kingman calls me and wants to know why we include the town of Nelson on the state weather map. He also wanted to know where it is.

I didn't even know we did have Nelson on the state weather map. But, sure enough, there it was, up there above Kingman. I'd never even heard of Nelson before.

So, with my reporter's instincts honed to a razor's edge, I immediately set out to find out why Nelson is on our weather map and quickly came to the truth of the matter: Nobody knows. I couldn't find anyone in the office who knew anything about it. I couldn't even find anyone who had ever heard of it.

Are you surprised by this? I'm not.

It turns out we have two Nelsons in Arizona: this Nelson and another Nelson somewhere down in Pima County. Who knew?

I couldn't find out anything about the Pima County Nelson, but the other one, which is in Coconino County, turned out to be semi-interesting, although not semi-interesting enough to be on *The Republic's* weather map, if you ask me.

Nelson is — or was — on Arizona 66 about 50 miles or so northeast of Kingman. A post office was established there in 1904, according to *Arizona Place Names*, and the town was named after Fred Nelson, who was a roadway superintendent for the railroad.

About the only thing left there now is the Chemical Lime Co. plant, which, not surprisingly, produces lime and is managed by Mike Staggs, who is a very nice guy.

According to Staggs, Nelson was quite the place in its day. It was a busy railroad town and a center for ranching and mining.

However, the railroads pulled out after World War II, and by the '70s, Nelson was pretty much gone. All that's left now are a few old buildings, the lime plant and the occasional curious tourist.

And, by the way, the forecast for Nelson this week is sunny with highs in the 60s.

A Q That Merits No A

November 22, 2002

Today's question: *Could you do a chart of the variables related to altitude? For instance, if we drive to the top of Mount Ord, it's about 7,500 feet high vs. 1,200 feet in Mesa. What horsepower drop would I expect at this altitude? Can you make a chart that would give the variables per 1,000 feet altitude for the following: temperature, pressure in pounds per square inch, boiling temperature of water, ultraviolet radiation? Please list the source of the data.*

Answer: Are you stoned?

Geez. You people.

Instead we shall take up a couple of questions that have come in recently regarding roadrunners.

When I go hiking at South Mountain, I usually see roadrunners, but recently I have not seen any. Do roadrunners migrate?

No, they don't migrate. It's possible, I suppose, that when the weather cooled, the stuff they eat, which is pretty much anything alive that is smaller than they are, relocated or changed habits, so maybe the roadrunners moved with their prey and that's why you're not seeing them where you usually do. Or maybe they just got tired of seeing your knobby old knees going down the trail.

We have a roadrunner that roosts in our carport. It is a friendly thing except for the occasion when it sneaked up behind my wife and scared her half to death. There's a question that is starting to obsess us though: How do you tell the difference between a male and female roadrunner?

Did you see that story in the paper the other day about Prince Charles and how he has servants who put the toothpaste on his toothbrush for him? I suppose it might be cool to be rich enough to have a servant or two, but don't you think that sooner or later you'd just want to say, "Hey, look. I can handle the toothpaste myself, OK? So get out of here and leave me alone?" I don't know. I guess that's Prince Charles' business and not mine.

As to the sex of your roadrunner: As far as I have been able to determine, one roadrunner looks much like another unless you are a roadrunner and then I guess you can tell the difference.

Maybe the females are slightly bigger, because female birds are often bigger than males, but unless you found a decidedly male roadrunner and compared it to the one in your carport, I suppose you wouldn't know.

Try this: If your carport roadrunner makes a shallow nest and lays some eggs in it, I'm betting it's a female. If it offers your wife a dead lizard or a snake that it has whomped against a rock for a while, it's probably a male and is trying to court your wife, in which case the three of you will have to decide how to handle the situation like mature adults.

Spaniards Weren't Stupid

December 12, 2002

Today's question: *If Arizona and New Mexico were both settled by the Spanish, why does New Mexico seem to have a much stronger Hispanic heritage than we do?*

That's a good one. For help on this I turned to good old Marshall Trimble, author, singer, teacher, Arizona state historian and all-around swell guy.

The answer in a nutshell is because the early Spanish settlers and explorers weren't completely stupid.

It starts in 1540 with Coronado, who wandered around the Southwest and up into Kansas for a couple of years looking for the fabled cities of gold, which, of course, he did not find. So he went home, where, according to legend, he found out his wife had been fooling around with another guy while he was out traipsing around, and eventually he died.

Then nothing much happened for 40 years or so because the Spanish had plenty to do in Mexico and, since there weren't any cities of gold here, they decided to stay home. They had to wait to forget, as Trimble put it.

So 40 years later a new generation of the Spanish got the exploring bug and headed north looking for treasure and settlement opportunities and even the Northwest Passage. The thought was it was someplace in northern New Mexico or southern Colorado. Those wacky Spaniards.

However, as noted, they weren't completely stupid. They looked at New Mexico, which had water in its rivers, especially the Rio Grande, and which had peaceable Pueblo Indians. And they looked at Arizona, which had hardly any water and had a lot of Native Americans, especially the Apaches, who tended to be on the crabby side when it came to the Spanish. Hmm, tough choice.

So they moved into New Mexico, founded some towns and settled down to farm and mine and so on.

Meanwhile, not much was going on in Arizona. Tucson was founded in 1775, but even when the Americans started turning up in the 1850s, the Spanish or Mexican population there was rather small, Trimble said. Tubac had been founded a few years earlier, but every now and then the Apaches wiped it out.

Eventually, the Spanish bought peace with the Apaches, but after Mexico gained its independence in 1812, it stopped payments and the Apaches went back to whacking people.

It wasn't until around the 1850s and 1860s, when miners and railroads started moving into Arizona, that the population started to grow and that population was mostly Anglo. Hence, all the good chilies come from New Mexico.

Valley Has Its Own Area 51
February 9, 2003

Today's question: *My friends and I often mountain-bike in the Dreamy Draw area. Recently one of the guys started talking about how a UFO crashed there in 1947 and was buried under the Dreamy Draw Dam. What's up with that?*

Well, I guess it depends on if you believe in UFOs or not. If you don't believe in UFOs, then this story is just hooey. If you do believe in UFOs, then the Dreamy Draw Dam was built to cover one up.

Personally, I'm not sure what I think about UFOs and ETs and all that stuff. They don't seem very likely, but on the other hand, it would explain a lot of my masters' behavior. And clothes. They just haven't learned our Earth ways yet.

But I digress.

The Dreamy Draw UFO story, as you might expect, has several variations. One has it that in 1947, about three months after the famous UFO incident in Roswell, N.M., a UFO crashed somewhere in the Dreamy Draw area. Another version has the spaceship setting down in that area but actually crashing about 10 miles away near a Cave Creek landfill.

Supposedly, the remains of its two passengers, described as about 4 ½ feet tall, were recovered. They were kept in some guy's freezer for a while and then taken away by the military.

And supposedly the reason the Army Corps of Engineers built the Dreamy Draw Dam was not for flood control, as you might suppose, but to bury the UFO. Do you know where the Dreamy Draw Dam is? If you're going north on the Squaw Peak Parkway, it's off to your right a bit above Northern Avenue.

I asked Ted Kester, who is in charge of the city's mountain preserves in that part of town, about this, and he said he'd heard the legend but couldn't recall anyone ever asking about it. So it's not exactly a mecca for ufologists.

You can find some stuff, not much, on the Internet about this matter, and it was mentioned in a 1952 book, *Behind the Flying Saucers* by Frank Scully.

I checked the newspaper files and didn't find too much on the subject. It probably was hushed up by my masters on orders from Uranus.

Mr. Cloud Knows His Chemistry
February 17, 2003

I am sorry, folks, but I do not know where you can find elderberries around here. I do not know how to determine how many degrees off plumb half a bubble would be. I do not know what those little dots on your ceiling are. I suspect they are flyspecks, but I don't know.

I also don't know why for sure I took up today's question. It involves numbers and formulas and stuff and little good ever comes from meddling with powerful forces such as those. Nonetheless, it had a certain appeal, I guess.

If clouds are full of water, they must be very heavy. How are they able to float in the sky like they do if they are so waterlogged?

I feel a need to sigh deeply at this point, but I am not sure why. Perhaps it is because we are going to have to discuss weight vs. density, and I always have trouble with that. Had I known it was going to come to this, I would have paid more attention during physics class or whatever class it was that that came up in.

First of all, you are correct. Clouds weigh a lot. A nice, fluffy, ordinary cumulus cloud of no particular distinction might weigh as much as 500,000 pounds. Big thunderheads can weigh tons and tons and tons.

If even a little innocuous-looking cloud were suddenly to plunge out of the sky and hit you on the head, you would be squished.

However, clouds do not just fall out of the sky. For one thing, they are held aloft by updrafts. Your ordinary raindrop is exceedingly small, so it doesn't take much of an updraft to suspend it in air. A raindrop doesn't fall until the water droplet or ice crystal has been bounced up and down in a cloud to the point where it gloms on to enough other drops or crystals and gets heavy enough to overcome the updraft.

Next: the density thing. Density is mass divided by volume. Write that down. Moist air — the air in a cloud, for example — is less dense than dry air.

Way up high in the sky where Mr. Cloud lives, there is a lot of oxygen and nitrogen, but up that high, they are both what you call diatomic. Instead of O and N, they are O_2 and N_2, which means they have atomic masses of 32 and 28 units, respectively.

Water vapor, on the other hand, is made of one oxygen atom and two hydrogen atoms. Hydrogen is very light, just one atomic unit, and oxygen, the non-diatomic brand, is 16 atomic units, which adds up to 18 atomic units.

Hence, assuming the temperature is equal, moist air is less dense than dry air and hence water vapor can float along in the air.

Worms Don't Mind The Wet
February 26, 2003

Just the other day, one of my masters walked right up to my cubicle, bold as brass, and started talking to me. So much for sheet plastic and duct tape. I'm going to have to think of something else. Dang.

No time to worry about that now because I have important news about worms. The last time it rained, I started getting calls from people who were wondering why they were finding all sorts of worms on their driveways and patios and so on. Three of my colleagues even asked me about this. One of them said that worms were crawling into her house.

I thought this was pretty dumb because everyone knows that when it rains and the ground gets saturated the worms come to the surface so they won't drown. So I said rude things to my colleagues and ignored the people who called to ask about this.

Well, it seems that I have to apologize to the callers I ignored. Not to my three colleagues, though. I'd rather die.

In the course of looking up something else, I came across an interview with one Mary Fauci, who is a worm researcher at Washington State University. It was at www.columbian.com.

Did you know that in parts of Oregon, Washington and Idaho they have a worm, the giant Palouse earthworm, that is 3 feet long or something like that? It's pink and white, and when you handle it, it gives off the aroma of lilacs. A pink and white 3-foot-long worm that smells like lilacs. Cool.

But I digress.

This is the deal about rain and drowning worms: Worms breathe through their skin. They take in oxygen through a bunch of minute blood vessels just under the surface of their skin. Fauci said worms can live for months in saturated soil if there is enough oxygen in the water.

The thing is that nobody seems to be quite sure why they surface when it rains. One theory is that the rain washes some kind of irritants into their burrows, chemicals or something.

Another idea is that it is a good opportunity for the worms to get out and look around. Worms can't take a lot of direct sunlight. So a rainy day gives them a good chance to get out of their burrows, surface, crawl around a bit, check out worm babes and so on, because obviously you are not going to meet a lot of other worms if you're living in a one-worm burrow.

When you think about it, the whole drowning thing didn't make sense anyway. If lots of worms were in danger of drowning every time it rained, eventually we'd run out of worms, with the exception of my masters.

There always seem to be enough of them to go around.

Oh, My Aching Fata Morgana

March 6, 2003

Answer me this, please:

How is it that a man — an average sort of gentleman of reasonable fitness and flexibility, a man who has neither unduly exerted himself nor sat idle all day, a person who perhaps on his good days might even generously be described as lithe — can go to bed feeling hale and fit and wake up the next day with a back so stiff and aching and sore that putting on pants takes time and socks are out of the question?

Does this seem right or reasonable? Or even fair? Well? Huh? Does it?

You think about that for a bit while I soldier on — noble lad! — with today's question.

On a cross-country trip, my husband and I started wondering about those "pool of water" reflections on the road ahead. What causes that?

These travelers have seen, as we all have, a very common mirage.

There are two kinds of mirages: inferior and superior. Inferior means the object is displaced downward. Superior is the other way around. The road thing is an inferior mirage.

On a sunny day the surface of the road and the air just above it get very hot. The air just above that is fairly cool in comparison.

Now, light travels faster through warm air than it does through cold air because warm air is less dense. Hence, when light hits that hot air just above the road surface at a certain angle, it changes speed and is bent upward.

As a result, the light that hits your eye shows you a patch of sky where the road should be, an inferior mirage. It is an optical illusion, a joke that light has played on your brain, a joke that light never seems to get tired of and that your brain falls for every time.

A superior mirage occurs when there is a layer of warm air over colder air, a temperature inversion. They are fairly common over snowfields or over large bodies of water where it might appear a boat is floating in the air.

Some people think that some UFO sightings in which the flying saucers seem to dart through the sky and vanish are really superior mirages caused by the refraction of automobile headlights. That makes sense.

There is also a very rare type of mirage called a "fata morgana," which is a combination of superior and inferior mirages that occurs only under certain atmospheric conditions. It is said to be quite something.

I could explain how those certain atmospheric conditions create a combination of superior and inferior mirages, but frankly I don't have the faintest idea.

Instead, I'm going to go try again to put my socks on. My feet are cold.

You Drive Me Up A Citrus Tree
March 16, 2003

A guy called me the other day and wanted to know if an orange feels pain when you peel it.

Normally, this would have been an occasion for me to put my head on my desk and sigh deeply, but for some reason this question cheered me greatly. You people just keep getting odder and odder. That's what I like about you.

Oranges do not feel pain when you peel them, OK? They're oranges, aren't they? Fruit. Disconnected from the tree. How are they going to feel pain? Where do you people get these ideas?

Be that as it may. Today we are going to discuss another citrus question. *I have three citrus trees: tangerine, orange and grapefruit. All have fruit and are blossoming. Does having ripened fruit on the trees harm the future crop?*

First, I would like to do my annual rant about citrus blossoms. I simply cannot abide that smell. There. That's taken care of for another year.

Now, as to the question: For help on this matter I turned to my pals at the University of Arizona Cooperative Extension. They are soooo smart over there. I wonder if I could just get my desk moved over to their office. It would spare me all those calls, and I bet there are good eats at the office potlucks. You newcomers especially should make use of them for your questions about gardening and stuff like that. The phone number is (602) 470-8086, and the Web address is http://ag.arizona.edu/maricopa. They're great.

So I put this ripe fruit/blossoms thing to Kelly Young, a program coordinator for urban horticulture, and she said there is no problem with the ripe fruit hanging around while the tree sets blossoms for the next crop.

"People don't need to worry about picking all the fruit off the trees to get a good set next year." Her very words.

In fact, some of the citrus is just now getting good. Young said that grapefruit in particular usually doesn't reach its full flavor until June or so. I didn't know that.

And while we're at it, if you didn't fertilize your citrus trees in February, you should be doing it now. Young said it's OK to fertilize trees that are still carrying ripe fruit. The fertilizer doesn't get sucked up into the fruit to make it taste funny.

As long as we're being all horticulture-ish, now also is the time to plant seeds for lima beans, snap beans, carrots, cucumbers, melons, pumpkins, onions, radishes, sunflowers, squash, corn and beets, although why anyone would want to use up perfectly good soil and water to grow a beet is beyond me.

Decision To Change Name Wise

April 6, 2003

Today's question: *What happened to the SH Mountains? I can't find them on any maps anymore.*

Nothing happened to them. It's not like they disappeared or something. It's just that over the years they got renamed, and rightly so.

They are now known as the Kofa Mountains, located about 70 miles northeast of Yuma.

The SH Mountains were so named back in the 1800s either by miners or soldiers who noticed that from a distance they resembled outhouses. I will leave it to you to figure out what SH stood for. Suffice it to say, it is not a word one would expect to read in this newspaper.

In the interest of delicacy, the SH range was also known over the years as the Short Horn or Stone House mountains until the mapmakers finally settled on Kofa.

There was a town of Kofa, in Yuma County, which took its name from the nearby King of Arizona mine, which used to mark its corporate possessions with the brand K of A.

The King of Arizona mine was discovered by Col. Charles Eichelberger in 1896. Over the next 14 years, the mine produced something like $3.5 million in gold ore, which, of course, was a lot of money in those days.

The post office in booming Kofa was opened in 1900 but closed in 1928.

As always in these matters, I turn for help to *Arizona Place Names* by Will Barnes and *Arizona Names: X Marks the Spot* by Byrd Howell Granger.

Wren Rarely Has Thorn In Its Side

April 30, 2003

The collective name for a group of butterflies is a flutter. One of you asked me that the other day, and I looked it up. That's that.

This leaves us plenty of space to discuss today's question, which, if you think about it, is pretty interesting.

How is it that cactus wrens don't impale themselves when they land on or nest in a saguaro or a cholla? Do they possess some kind of tiny body armor to protect against getting poked?

Randy Bapp, a biologist at the state Game and Fish Department, said every now and then, the cactus wrens do get impaled on saguaro spines or are found on the ground with a ball of cholla needles stuck in their breast.

I'm not sure why, but I find this kind of reassuring. It's not that I like the idea of the little creatures suffering or whatever. I don't know. I guess I just like the idea of them messing up sometimes.

However, for the most part, cactus wrens and other desert animals have learned to live with thorns. Bapp called it "behavioral and functional adaptation."

It is, as he pointed out, the same reason a coyote can run through a patch of desert where a dog can't go, or at least not a dog with any sense. Or why a pack rat can carry a cholla ball in its mouth without harm, or why a hawk can perch on a saguaro in perfect comfort. Actually, a hawk has leathery feet and tries to plant its toes between the spines.

And there is the matter of weight. A cactus wren, although good-sized for a wren, is light enough to perch on cactus spines without applying enough force to get impaled.

The cactus wren is a fairly interesting bird. It is, of course, our state bird, but I doubt if that means much to your average cactus wren. It's not like you see them wearing little bola ties or anything.

Mystery Castle Is Weirdness

May 10, 2003

Today's column is strictly newcomer's stuff, so if you have lived here for more than a few years, and think you know your way around, you should find something else to do.

The garage wants cleaning, I bet, or maybe you should go for a hike while the weather is still so pleasant.

Speaking of which, did I ever tell you about my masters and the first-100-degree-day story? A few weeks ago the lords of darkness told me to write a first-100-degree-day story to run on such-and-such a date, even though we had not yet hit 100, nor was there any sign we would do so soon. The reason? They had by-damn scheduled the story for that date, and they were by-damn going to run it on that date.

Someone must have adjusted their meds, because they eventually dropped this plan, but I thought the wage slaves among you would appreciate the story.

Anyway, I have a confession. I have lived here for a long time, and until just the other day, I had never visited the Mystery Castle. I now deeply regret these wasted years.

Eight hundred E. Mineral Road. South of Dobbins Road, off Central Avenue. Five bucks, cheaper for seniors and the kiddies. Thursday through Sunday, 11 a.m. to 4 p.m. Closed during July, August and September.

Mystery Castle was built between 1930 and 1945 by one Boyce Luther Gulley, who abandoned his wife and daughter in the Northwest and moved down here to recover from tuberculosis. He ended up dying of cancer, so I guess the desert air did him some good.

Gulley spent 15 years building an 18-room, 8,000-square-foot house out of rocks, relics, broken glass, odd bits of wood and metal, antiques, junk and crap, and I mean junk and crap in the very finest Valley 101 sense of both words.

This is what I like about this place: It's very odd.

For another thing, it is a memory of the days when you could come out here and claim a piece of desert and build whatever kind of whacko thing you felt like building, and it wouldn't have to be acres of red-tile-roofed, cookie-cutter houses in some gated development with a made-up, Spanish-sounding name and postage-stamp-size lots with a view from the dining room window of your neighbor's block fence.

Sorry. I got a little cranky there.

Anyway, I know you guys, and you should go see the Mystery Castle as soon as possible. It's just the sort of thing that would appeal to you people.

Don't Fret, Just Have A Good Time

July 16, 2003

This is what I'm thinking: I'm thinking the monsoon can't get here soon enough. It's not just that we need the rain. It's that you people need something new to occupy your thoughts, to keep you busy.

You people are thinking too much, worrying too much. I think it comes from being cooped up by the heat. A nice, brisk monsoon storm would get you out in the front yard, watching the lightning, talking to the neighbors, getting some fresh air. It would be good for you.

As witness to this too-much-thinking thing, I have at hand a question from a guy who wants to know why they don't make bacon out of beef. This seems to be weighing on his mind. Actually, you can make bacon out of beef, although I've never had it.

And today's two related questions clearly show symptoms of excessive worrying.

Remember those awful fires in mountains of old tires that pour smoke into the air and burn forever? Suppose we had a car fire on rubberized asphalt, that stuff with shredded old tires in it. Would it catch it on fire? Would the freeway burn for days or even weeks?

And:

I have read in the past that while driving my vehicle, the tires release particles into the air, contributing to air pollution. My question is: Does the rubberized asphalt being applied to the Valley freeways contribute to air pollution?

See what I mean? You guys are thinking too much.

I put these matters to Matt Burdick, who knows all about stuff like this because he is a spokesman for the state Department of Transportation. He said not to worry.

About 10,000 old tires are recycled for every mile of rubberized asphalt that gets put down. However, according to Burdick, the overall amount of rubber in the asphalt is fairly small.

The rubber gets liquefied into an oil mixture and then is mixed in with the asphalt. That oil mixture accounts for about 10 percent of the weight of the stuff that ends up on the road, and only about 1 or 2 percent of that is rubber, Burdick said.

It is true that there is a certain amount of tire dust in the air. I think I did a column about that once. However, in the case of rubberized asphalt, the rubber is encapsulated in the asphalt so passing cars are not churning it into the air, Burdick said.

The same goes for fire. The rubber is locked into the asphalt. It isn't going to burn. Don't worry about it.

Now, the forecast calls for a 20 percent chance of rain tonight, so let's keep our fingers crossed.

Meanwhile, try to follow my example: Stop thinking.

Afterword

So, what did you think? I hope you liked it. I had to read the entire text of this book about 18 times in the course of a month or so before publication and frankly, I'm sick to death of it. I think it's best taken in bits and pieces. Still, as I said, I hope you enjoyed it.

Did you notice that nowhere in the book did I mention that my daughters need new shoes? Oh, I guess they could get by for another year sharing a pair, but still, it would be nice if they could each have their own, don't you think? So while I appreciate you buying the book, maybe you'd like to think of buying another copy to send to Aunt Sally in St. Paul or whatever. Or, if you bought enough of them, you might use them to make a lovely planter or whatever, or maybe you could do that origami thing.

Actually, my publisher is making me write this part. I thought my *Republic* masters were money-grubbers, but this guy could teach them a trick or two. And his wife seems so nice. I guess you just never know.

Anyway, you can buy extra copies of this book direct from the publisher at www.claythompsonbooks.com and there's also a link there for sending in questions to "Valley 101" and for reading the present day's column, providing I still have a job when you read this. The publisher set up that Web site. Like I could set up a Web site? Shaa.

If you don't care for the Web you can always send a check to the publisher—Primer Publishers, 5738 N. Central Ave., Phoenix, AZ 85012. They can also take credit card orders over the phone at 800-521-9221. I don't think you can just go by there and get a copy. They'd probably put the Dobermans on you. In any event, the book is $14.95, tax is $1.21 (for those sold in Arizona), and shipping is $2.50, so that's $18.66 per copy. It would make you weep to know how little I get out of that, but still every few pennies towards the girls' new shoes helps.